# SONNETS

# # S O N N E T S

*Treating of such*
## DIVERSE MATTERS
*as*
## KIM KARDASHIAN,
## TINDER & PIKACHU

*Lucien Young*

**unbound**

First published in 2019

Unbound
6th Floor Mutual House, 70 Conduit Street, London W1S 2GF
www.unbound.com

© Lucien Young, 2019

Illustrations © Ollie Mann, 2019

Text design by Patty Rennie

A CIP record for this book is available
from the British Library

ISBN 978-1-78352-820-2 (hardback)
ISBN 978-1-78352-828-8 (ebook)

Printed in Great Britain by CPI Group (UK)

1 3 5 7 9 10 8 6 4 2

# A NOTE FROM THE POET

Dear reader, I consider thee a friend,
⠀⠀Therefore I urge thee: do not feel compelled
To read this book of verses start to end,
Lest they into some senseless mess should meld.
On nerdish themes my mind is wont to brood
Such that thy wasted time thou might'st begrudge;
The baffled soul who ne'er *The West Wing* viewed
Would through the corresponding sonnet trudge.
Thus do I bid he turn to page eleven
Who would of Queen Beyoncé gladly read,
While she who Netflix doth declare a heaven
Should right away to one-and-twenty speed.
⠀⠀Pray see my work as but a playful pool:
⠀⠀Dip in and out, as doth your fancy rule.

# CONTENTS

# INTRO

I know what thou art thinking: why did I
These sonnets write in twenty seventeen?
Do I imagine there are people keen
To give my poor pentameter a try?
And, furthermore, who do I hope will buy
A book that doth the noble form demean
With subject matter frivolous, obscene
And quite impossible to dignify?
In truth, I needed it to occupy
My febrile brain, for what a year it's been.
I thought I could, with verse iambic, pry
Some sense from nonsense, and our modern scene
    Depict and mock, while using 'thee' and 'thy'
    In pages fit to rest by thy latrine.

# KIM KARDASHIAN

## *1.*

When I beheld upon my laptop screen
The best and brightest of our earthly stars
As cover girl of *Paper* magazine,
With gloves and pearls and glist'ning, global arse,
Then did my heart with foreign feelings flare,
For little had I known erotic passion
Ere I had glimpsed thy shining derriere
And learned thy gilded name, O Kim Kardashian!
But thereon grieved my soul, for I did think
Of how thy form empixelled might remain,
That, IRL, my lips might never drink
A glass of thy butt-balancèd champagne.
    I need thee, Kim; oh prithee do not let
    My heart be broken like the internet!

## 2.

Thou Aphrodite Kallipygos! Thou
    Proud-buttocked cynosure of ev'ry eye!
Thou shining mistress of the here and now,
Thou queen Armenian, thou mystery!
Thy grace exceedeth Khloe's far, and Kourtney
Rejoiceth not to glimpse thy Twitter count;
Some fifty million followers support me
When I do argue thou art paramount.
Thou cardinal Kardashian! My love!
How doth thy broadcasts gladden mine antenna,
Thou TV star, whom I admire above
Kris, Kendall, Kylie, even Caitlyn Jenner!
    Thou art a goddess, and thy tape with Ray J
    Doth get me off, just as thy dad did OJ.

### 3.

Wherefore do fools thy great renown dismiss
  And jeer that thou art famed for being
famed?
They claim thy wealth unyoked to talent is,
That of thy fortune thou should'st be ashamed.
Know they not of thy vaunted app, Kimoji,
Or thy bestselling book, of selfies made?
Think they the giddy sums that E! bestows thee
Reflect not well thy powers to persuade?
Why claim they thou art symptom of an age
Of frippery, an Instagramming whore?
Art thou not kindred of old Betty Paige,
Monroe and Grable and Zsa Zsa Gabor?
    I will not grant to watch thee is obnoxious:
    'Tis so to mock thee, or upbraid thy watchers.

## 4.

Kanye, can ye hear this lover's moan?
For, while my heart doth linger on the shelf,
Thou hast beguiled my darling of her own,
Thou rapper rapt in nothing but thyself!
Thou art a knavish braggart, and thy verse
Time's with'ring hand shall rightfully diminish.
I tailored swift these lines thy name to curse
And, having more, I pray thou let'st me finish!
But why? Such barren words avail me naught
And vengeful verse my sorrow scarce appeases;
My love, alas, is now by Yeezy taught
And pledges her immortal soul to Yeezus.

    For, like a setting sun, my Kim hath blest
    With golden light the undeserving West.

## 5.

These sonnets jest, dear K, for well I grasp
That this, my love, shall not returnèd be.
In dreams alone I shall thy backside clasp;
I know thee from, not in, reality.
Thou art a creature far beyond my aim,
Yet still it pains me when each day I glance
At websites that thine exploits doth proclaim
And magazines that bear thy countenance.
But one sweet notion keeps me from despair:
'Tis for thine image, not thyself, I fell,
Thine image, which endureth everywhere
And never shall my yearning eyes repel!
    While I love this, thine all-pervading double,
    No earthly hindrance may my loving trouble.

# DARTH VADER

Thou art of villains paramount, my lord:
A black and gasping emblem of thy kind.
Thine is the helmet, cape and laser sword.
Thou chokest henchmen merely with thy mind!
Thou wert of thy limbs pruned, poor Anakin,
On Mustafar, then hurled in hellish lava,
Yet still thou send'st the rebels panicking.
I would be proud to say thou wert my father!
And though unyielding death may dim thy star
In cruel defiance of thy Dark Side might,
By this fair stanza, thou preservèd are
As though encased in frozen carbonite.
    Dread Sith, I pray that thou, of voice unnerving,
    Shalt never find my lack of faith disturbing.

# EMINEM

ow shall I marshal fourteen lines to tell
Thee what, in teenage years, thy dope
   rhymes meant?
No other rapper in thy bourn may dwell,
For, Eminem, thou art preeminent!
I learned thy LPs' sickest flows by heart,
Then did, in hope to more adore thee, delve
Into thy diss tracks' cruel, exquisite art
And thy collaborations with D12.
But as I aged, so came I to revile
The homophobic slurs that thou wouldst level
And winced to think the Shakespeare of *8 Mile*
Misogynist — a pinched, peroxide devil!
   Yet still will I, for all my earthly span,
   On thee obsess as though my name were Stan.

# WALTER WHITE

O Heisenberg, did not that shaven head
Contain the thought thy wicked deeds could scar thee?
Thou should'st have taught thy chemistry instead
Of cooking crystal in some antique RV.
But no, thou wouldst be Albuquerque's king,
Thine empire built on meth heads and thy madness,
Face off 'gainst Tuco and Gustavo Fring
And bring thy boring family naught but sadness.
Thou in the desert stood'st, thy pants near soiled,
Thou didst, for seasons six, earn our reproof.
Now, Ozymandias, all thy works lie spoiled,
Like to a pizza hurlèd on the roof.
　　Thy barrelled cash could not thy soul enrich:
　　Such were the limits of thy science, bitch!

# BEYONCÉ

Queen B, thy honeyed tones and sweet melisma
Doth slay such other loves as I have faced.
Thou mad'st me swoon with thy onstage charisma
And laugh with joy when thou *Goldmember* graced.
Thou chartest thy career in steps judicious,
Thy beauty could defeat the wit of Shelley.
Whene'er I see thy body bootylicious
I think myself unready for this jelly.
But pray do not pretend thou lovest Jay-Z
When all the watching world can sense the rift.
Say not thou stand'st by — and the thought dismays
    me —
The churl thy sister twatted in a lift!
    Take thou my heart, or else thou hast beguiled
    The world of love, and of our destined child.

# PIKACHU

Good friend, thou see'st this lonely seeker through
His long travails, his quest to catch them all
And I am blessed that thou, dear Pikachu,
Dost rest in my unworthy Poké Ball.
I love thy spotted cheeks and bolt-like tail;
With thine electric form I have no gripe,
For thy aggressions proveth, without fail,
Super effective 'gainst all Water type.
And though some trainers may of Mewtwo boast,
Or hold their Venusaur in high regard,
I would not trade thee for a Gyarados,
A Dragonite, or shiny Charizard.
    Why should I yearn for some dull Jolteon?
    Thou art the paragon of Pokémon.

# BINGEING

Like to that television show I binge
    Whilst laid in bed, these eyes abjuring rest,
Whose thrills allow no other to impinge
On those few hours of mine with freedom blessed,
Such is my love; thou art my sole download,
The one Must See for which my passion burns.
When credits roll, 'Just one more episode!'
I cry, enraptured by thy twists and turns.
Yet thou art greater still, for series finish,
Or else decline and lose their former spark;
But seasons' march shall not thy grace diminish,
Nor shall thy loveliness e'er jump the shark.
    While men still breathe and God maintains
      His station,
    This love of ours shall ne'er know cancellation.

# TINDER

## *1.*

My heart aflame, I swipe with finger deft
    The myriad nymphs who dance before my sight,
And, for each one I banish to the left,
My horniness doth hurl a thousand right.
I think myself a Roman emperor
Whose twitching thumb commands the fatal strike.
Shall this new girl feel my contempt for her
Or else be humbled by my super like?
Then I despair, perceiving what the catch is:
My profile pic these girls approveth not
And soon enough my few enticing matches
Reveal themselves a false and thieving bot.
    Then do I pity those I leftward nudged,
    For as one judges, so must one be judged.

## 2.

Untender Tinder, how thou feedst my doubt
 When thine erotic Rolodex I spin
And see each face congealed in fish-like pout
And ev'ry bio boasting love of gin.
Too oft my lust is cruelly thrown off kilter
When women of their basic pastimes shout,
Or else their beauties burden with that filter
That doth impose on them a canine snout.
And yet, alas, I vainly make this fuss:
I still shall swipe, albeit with teeth gritted,
And, though I may refrain from Tinder Plus,
I wholly lack the fortitude to quit it.

    For I prefer to burn in Tinder's hell
    Than e'er approach a lady IRL.

## 3.

Full oft have I thine algorithm cursed
And scorned thy slick and faithless interface,
Or else thy users' tawdry tics rehearsed,
Thou base usurper of romance's place!
But now my heart thy kind forgiveness begs,
For, though I stand by ev'ry censure made,
And rue each squandered swipe through dating's
    dregs,
Each sparkless match, each compliment I paid,
On thee I found her: she who lights my life,
Who from love's endless game would set me free.
And, though thou mayst have yielded years of strife,
Thou, pocket Pandarus, broughtst her to me
    At whose sweet touch all former shames collapse.
    Thus, Tinder, I proclaim thee king of apps!

# FACEBOOK

Say not thou art my friend, when thou
  hast broke
My heart a thousand times with careless talk
And daily dost that injured organ poke
By letting me my former girlfriends stalk.
Because of thee, my fingers are as traitors
Each time they rush to type a comment lame,
Or else betray me in some try-hard status
That shames my feed as it doth feed my shame.
And though I swear I shall abjure thy site,
Thou Book of Faces, granting thus my heart ease,
I check thee still with joyless appetite
(And plus, in fairness, thou art good for parties).
  Therefore I am, each day, of freedom shorn
  By thee, Mark Zuckerberg's unholy spawn.

# AUSTIN POWERS

What need have I of Craig or Connery,
   Whose dark and dismal exploits doth
   dismay me?
Such sullen spies are but thy Mini-Me;
Thou art incomparably more groovy, baby.
Thou shagg'st and sport'st thy Union Jack pants well
And, when I glimpse that patriotic rump,
Then love of country in my chest doth swell,
Like to a penis in a Swedish pump.
Fear not that Dr Evil shall prevail,
Try as he might thy mojo to oppose,
Nor shall Time triumph where the Fembots fail
And bring thy swinging antics to a close.
   For thine example cannot be outlasted:
   Thy name looms larger than thy foe,
      Fat Bastard.

# PLASTIC SURGERY

Sweet surgeon, fetch thy scalpel and syringe,
   For with abundant faults I am bestowed:
Smooth out those lines that on my brow impinge,
Relieve these eye-bags of their heavy load.
Then lend some strength to this unmanly jaw,
Erase the scars of acne's cruel eruption,
Each tufted mole remove, lost youth restore,
And purge my back fat with thy liposuction!
Yet no — I pray, withhold thy anaesthetic.
My mind is changed: imperfect shall I stay,
For though my form is pasty and pathetic,
My love proclaims she loves me anyway.
    Thus is self-hate cast off by means fantastic
    And, having love, I have no need of plastic.

# NETFLIX

How I do thrill at thy great panoply!
Thine endless content doth my heart content.
Ne'er do I grudge thy small subscription fee,
Much less the countless hours on thee spent.
For when I would my thirsting laptop slake,
Assemblest thou the songs of sundry bards:
One eve I shall of *Stranger Things* partake
The next of *Narcos*, *Love* or *House of Cards*.
Alas, at times thy wares are so arousing
I cannot choose, and, vainly scrolling on,
I waste my day a thousand programmes browsing
And lose the chance to watch a single one.
    Man's heart, though lacking naught, still
        wanteth more
    And thus a wealth of choice doth make us poor.

# GAME OF THRONES

In Westeros, three noble houses feud
Called Lannister, Targaryen and Stark.
These lords and ladies in their towers brood
On ancient conflicts and betrayals dark,
While I, poor viewer, wonder why this show
Hath such a surfeit of protagonists.
Each hour brings more, although I scarcely know
Who that blonde woman with the dragon is!
But still I find, when seasons start to bore,
That Maesters Benioff and Weiss will push
Onscreen some bosomy medieval whore
With quite anachronistic lack of bush.

    Thus am I kept a sedulous downloader,
      Enduring endless scenes of Bran and Hodor.

# MRS SLOCOMBE

Imperious mistress, thou of mad-hued hair,
  Full often on thy form mine eyes have perved.
Fain would I be thy servant, and with care
Ensure thine ev'ry need was being served.
When thy great beauty graced the BBC,
Thou didst with ease outshine the fair Miss Brahms.
And still the question lingers: art thou free
To spend a lifetime in my loving arms?
Saleswoman cruel! Wouldst thou deny this bloke,
Who would quite gladly give his life so that
He might but once thy famous pussy stroke?
(And, no, I make not ref'rence to thy cat.)
    O Mrs Slocombe, how thy name doth trick,
    For when I think on thee, I come too quick!

# SNOOP DOGG

Let others laud their Tupacs and their Ices,
  Both Cube and T, their Biggies and their Dre-s.
Thou art more cool, thou rap game Dionysus,
Enshrouded in thy weed-cloud's shimm'ring haze.
Fain would I share a gin and juice with thee,
Whilst thou recounted great and pimpish deeds,
Then proudly toast the D-O-double-G
My blunt bereft of stems or sticks or seeds!
O, heed not thou those wack, allergic churls
Who call thee old, or by thy chronic marred,
Or say thy verse on 'California Gurls'
Doth mean thou art from O.G. status barred,
    For while the critics chide and haters grizzle
    Thou Snoop remain'st: the big boss Dogg,
        for shizzle.

# DOCTOR WHO

My love is like the Doctor, who doth save
The world each week: my love shuns not
the chase,
Nor is my love to earthly rules a slave,
But doth traverse the bounds of Time and Space.
My heart I have thee rendered; thine my heart is,
Thus double hearts doth beat in single breast.
My love of thee, proportioned like the TARDIS,
Is vaster than its outside might attest.
Like members of the Gallifreyan race,
The fleeting years cannot my love destroy.
It doth endure, though it may change its face
And spend unhappy ages as McCoy.
    Time's not our lord, my love, for passions great
    Not even Daleks may exterminate.

# LONDON

Thou mistress cruel! Thou dost mistreat me so.
Thou art unfriendly, dirty, rude and grave.
Though I admire thy grandeur, thou dost show
No corresponding love to me, thy slave.
I have not means within thy heart to dwell;
That central part disdains the likes of me,
But still I strive each day my soul to sell
That I might slum in thy periphery.
And yet, when I resolve from thee to 'scape
My will doth quickly fail. What should I do?
In some poor hamlet an existence scrape,
Where jobs are scarce and strangers talk to you?
   Thy loss imagined turns my veins to ice
   (Though lots of people tell me Brighton's nice).

# THE WOMEN OF X-MEN

Which female mutant matches best my love?
      Shall for a blazing Phoenix I thee take,
Whose mind all other minds doth soar above,
Or Storm, whose changing tempers tempests make?
Sometime thou putst on aspects like Mystique,
Or else the diamond form of Emma Frost;
Like Kitty Pryde, no bound'ry can thee pique;
Like Scarlet Witch, ne'er should thy charms
      be crossed.
But I know thou art Rogue: thy power's bourn
Containeth skill of all thy diverse peers;
Thy touch doth leave me weak, of vigour shorn,
While thou dost stronger grow with passing years.
      Thou art uncanny, love: I am thy captive;
      The great Magneto ne'er was more attractive.

# WOLVERINE

If thou art Rogue, then I, my love, am Logan,
The loner also known as Wolverine,
For, like his bones, my love cannot be broken
As though it bore an adamantium sheen.
Thy scornful looks may cut me deeper far
Than blades the Silver Samurai doth wield,
But fear I neither fatal blow nor scar
For when thou smil'st, I am as swiftly healed.
And yet my meagre claws cannot defend
Against thy changing moods: ay, there's the rub.
Sometime thou art my foe, sometime my friend;
Like Sabretooth, I cannot trust thee, bub.
    I would thee ken, but no one of my sex
    Shall know thy mind, not e'en Professor X.

# MAD MEN

Men who have secrets in their doleful eyes,
  Which speak of old misfortune and
    of danger,
May sweet contentment deftly advertise,
While to their hearts it doth remain a stranger.
And though they don fulfilment's drapery
And fill an office in some gleaming tower
And smoke and drink and do adultery,
They still doth dread the self-reflecting hour.
O Don, thy name's a fraud, thy home a shambles;
Thou art aware the future is not thine,
But rather Peggy's, Sally's and Pete Campbell's,
Who thee observe as looks and lungs decline.
  Too well thou knowest where thy soul doth dwell:
  Life's changeless, ever-changing carousel.

# TEXTING

## *1.*

I have thy number, but know not thy heart,
    Thus I resolve a flirty text to send.
Should I put 'hey' or 'what's up' at the start?
A kiss or sly emoji at the end?
Alas, each text seems trite and poorly phrased,
Naught but the trifle of a dullard's hand;
No sooner are they written than erased,
As though I write my lines upon the sand.
Some twenty efforts later, I despair
And at the iPhone's empty screen I blink,
When suddenly my muse doth heed my prayer
And I these words peck out: 'Fancy a drink?'
    Then, thinking that this draft cannot be bettered,
    I send the text, and instantly regret it.

## 2.

The bubble grey emerges, three small dots
Declare that thou dost fashion thy reply
And, lo, my brow is slicked, my stomach knots,
For soon thy precious words shall fill mine eye.
Whate'er thine answer be, I need it now,
Whether it yield me joy or endless night,
But as I doth some hopeful thought allow
Then — woe! — thy bubble disappeareth quite.
Like to the silver cloud, that, hanging o'er
Drought-stricken land, is by the wind dispersed
And granteth not the life-preserving shower
That souls below had prayed would end their thirst,
    Thus am I by this present absence vexed:
    Thou didst, with phone in hand, choose not
       to text.

## 3.

Long, anxious hours I wait, which do deny
My text an answer. Thus descends the night,
And sleeplessly I think on thy reply
Which may my dream of love reward or blight.
Wilt thou assent, but by the second pint,
A mention of thine unknown boyfriend drop,
Then show me photos of some muscled giant
Describing sex until I bid thee stop?
Might thy reply a drink forbid, for thou
Dost merely see me as a lovely friend,
Then pile thy neut'ring laurels on my brow
Till I do pray for mortal journey's end?
    Or wilt thou all my earthly hopes dismiss
    By texting that vile phrase: 'new phone,
        who dis'?

## 4.

Two days have passed; four dozen hours marred
By thy monastic silence, mistress cruel,
Whose faintest echo to my calling heart
Had caused these scalding agonies to cool.
So wherefore dost thou tarry? Tak'st thou pride
In this, my pain, which proveth thine allure?
But then I think that maybe thou hast died
(Which thought I might more happily endure).
Then, on the toilet, as I Twitter browse,
Thy text appears: 'Sure babe, wen's gud, 2nite?'
And all is joy. Mine easement e'en allows
That I forgive thy sloppy spelling quite.
For though 'tis brief, I think thy text as grand
As any epic that these eyes have scanned.

# DICK PIC

My far-off love a dick pic doth request.
'Tis not a prospect at which I rejoice,
But having photos of my love undressed
Delighted in, I scarcely have a choice.
And so, reluctantly, I whip it out:
The dick part's easy — what about the pic?
Which cam'ra angle best befits the snout?
Which filter flatters most the veinèd stick?
What if my love should giggle at my labour,
While all her friends partake of sneaky peeks?
Might I be hacked and see my fleshy sabre
Fall in the fearful grasp of WikiLeaks?
    I scan the poor result of all my graft:
    A nest of hair beneath a blurry shaft.

# MORRISSEY

Thou wert a charming man, back in the days
    When Thatcher reigned and all thy fans
    were young.
Thou met'st the camera with thy sullen gaze
And heavenwards thy gladioli swung.
Thou wert a handsome devil, lithe and dark;
Thy lyrics rang in ev'ry teenage journal.
Thou didst life save while singing like a lark
Of girlfriends comatose and lights eternal.
But now thou add'st three decades to thy sum
And each new interview doth make the charge
That thou, my youth's dear poet, hast become
A xenophobe; a warbling, Manc Farage.

   O Moz, my youth is gone, and so art thou!
   How fleeting be days past! How soon is now!

# NICOLA STURGEON

I was to nationalism's charm a virgin
  Before I heard thy fervent Scottish trill;
Now swimmest thou in my esteem, Ms Sturgeon,
Which element I pray doth suit thy gill.
Thou leapst above that other, lesser fish
Who in the SNP once played thy part.
Thou art the finest leader it could wish
And to its cleaving cause a blessing art.
Let Caledonia flee from English traps!
No Union doth this heart desire but ours;
To keep thy love I should the world collapse,
A thousand planets sunder from their stars.
    Let ev'ry molecule its bonds release,
      So long as our true bond may never cease.

# Hannibal Lecter

Thou dost consume my thoughts, thou
  bon viveur,
Of serial killers serially the best;
Beside thee Michael Myers seems a boor
And Jason Voorhees but a panting pest.
While thou dost languish in thy scanty cell,
Oft prodded by the dreadful Dr Chilton,
Still in thy mental palace mayst thou dwell,
Its lib'ry filled with works of Blake and Milton.
But do not waste thy words, my dapper darling,
On fools whose intellect shall never cut it,
Like that poor rube thou callest Agent Starling,
Who may not e'en compel the lambs to shut it.
     O Hannibal, thy deeds shall e'er enchant me
     (Though thou wouldst eat my liver with chianti).

# AMERICAN PIE

## *1.*

From Cleopatra to the Trojan Helen
To fair Godiva (she of Peeping Tom),
Nor hist'ry, nor the vasty world we dwell in,
May boast one fine as thee, O Stifler's Mom!
No other goddess may thy bust eclipse,
No nymphish horde contains a brow more fair,
Venus herself doth envy thou those lips
And Midas ne'er had gold to match thy hair.
I well remember how, at movie's end,
Thou cam'st into thy rec room, finding Finch,
And thinking him thy jockish offspring's friend,
Engaged the novice in erotic clinch.

    Yea, in that instant was my young heart pilfered,
    Who, prior to thee, had never of a MILF heard.

## 2.

If music be the food of love, then thou
   Must be the modern Mozart or Debussy,
For thou, Michelle, didst that one time allow
(Ye gods!) a band camp flute inside thy pussy.
Thus love and music give me food for thought,
Thou flame-haired fox, who seemed, at first, naive,
But soon the tender art of loving taught
To Jim, that ere to Nadia did cleave.
Then, from the spark of thine initial bedding,
The all-consuming fire of love did grow;
I loved thee in *Pie 2*, still more in *Wedding*
(Though to *Reunion* I declined to go).
      O sexy nerd, who did upon me stamp
      An endless yearning for that place, band camp!

*3.*

O Nadia, thou sultry immigrant,
    Might I on thy self-pleasuring intrude?
Thou bidst me strip: I gladly do assent,
Though we may be on common webcam viewed.
Let Blink-182 deride my dance!
They can but dream to have thee in their sheets
Or slip a questing finger down thy pants
As I do now, which hairless softness greets.
But then — oh God! — my twitching member spends
Before I may thy sweet enclosure know
And, to the anguish of my watching friends,
I likewise squander on the second go.
    O long-awaited joy, 'tis surely some
    Mistake that thou shouldst prematurely come!

# CROWDFUNDING

How like a modern Sisyphus I feel
    While writing yet another promo tweet,
Or else more emails, in which I appeal
To everyone I ever chanced to meet.
How hard it is! How utterly unsuited
Am I to so American a task;
My Facebook is unfriended, tweets are muted,
Warm friends turn cold when I for pledges ask.
But still, though self-hate burns and fingers ache,
I fain would place before the public eye
This foolish book of mine and, for its sake,
Shall keep on plugging till the day I die.
    So chuck a tenner in my beggar's cup:
    'Twould be the quickest way to shut me up.

# BREXIT

Thou dost disdain my heart, which loves
thee true;
Thus, in the cause of loving's termination,
Thou play'st the Britain to my heart's EU
And dost reject my tender regulation.
Why cravest thou love's bondage to escape?
Who filled thine outraged ear with blatant lies?
I would not change thy damn bananas' shape,
Nor do I thy soul's sovereignty despise.
'Tis true our tender union has its flaws
But must we then break up? Think'st not thou might
Adopt my reformation as thy cause
And save me sorrow and a decade's spite?
  No, thou wouldst rob the U from my EU
  And I, much like thy passport, must be blue.

# NIGEL FARAGE

A red-faced, toad-like, drunk and boorish bore,
    Thou didst thy party brew from
        England's dregs
And in the public cup contrived to pour
A mixture sprung from old and rotten kegs.
Long has that draught been with us, that
    which heated
Teutonic breasts within the Munich beer hall
And now has Britain of her future cheated,
As thou didst whisper in her drunken earhole.
Then, finding her hungover, thou didst face
Away, and didst thine injured land insult,
Insisting those who loved our global place
Should graciously accept this vile result.
    We never shall accept, but e'er despise it
    And thou shalt pay, for he who Brexit, buys it.

# JACK BAUER

O hero horological, how I
Did worship thee! How thou didst see
me through
Long teenage years, thou gravel-throated spy,
Who bravely battled 'longside CTU!
'Tis true I worried, on the other hand,
That audiences American should list
To watch the tiny Kiefer Sutherland
Beat up some hulking, brown-skinned terrorist.
But I such fascist leanings did ignore
And soon forgave thy pleading torture's case,
For it were greater torture to abjure
Thy blazing guns and ever-snarling face.
  E'en now my fancy doth thy features show me,
  Contorted in a scream of 'DAMMIT, CHLOE!'

# A Rapper's Reverie

O for a cup of sizzurp! Thou dost rank
    Above all party drugs that I have known.
Fain would I pair with thee, kind purple drank,
A bag of weed in California grown!
Or else some molly, in whose gorgeous throes
I should this club regard with eager eye
And seek the beauty of big-booty hoes,
Who might bestow more pleasure 'pon my high.
Yea, let me take my joy while I am able,
For soon draws in the dull and dreadful morrow
Of interviews, long meetings with the label
And all the rap game's many fonts of sorrow.
    I heed these not — tonight I gladly sup
    On sweetest lean, and soon am fuckèd up.

# DAVID BOWIE

Starman, Major Tom, Aladdin Sane!
Thou of a thousand faces, all thine own!
Chameleonic change didst thou attain,
While in each mask revealing David Jones:
A London boy who dreamt of life on Mars,
Who sold the world on strangeness and the queer,
Who sang of heroes, fame and crashing cars,
And gave all earthly freaks a cause to cheer.
Although thy hits in ev'ry jukebox spun,
Thou never ceased to ask, 'Where are we now?'
Nor ever deemed thy self-invention done,
But wove more laurels for thy lightning brow.
     Thou star, who over forty years did pass
     Through Ziggy, Thin White Duke and Lazarus!

# E.L. JAMES

Great pain doth yield me pleasure: hence thy pen
  Is pleasure's instrument; its clumsy stroke
Lasheth my taste, and I do glory when
I on thy massive solecisms choke.
Although thy Muse doth most ineptly tell
These tales of Mr Grey and Anastasia,
I heaven find in literary hell,
While other readers pray for euthanasia.
Thus, conquered by thine unerotic prose,
Which eagerly the English language maims,
I have a life of constant bondage chose,
To thee and thy sweet cruelty, Mistress James:
    My queen, who doth in gilded mansion sit
    And paint the world with fifty shades of shit!

# CONTACTLESS

I wave my plastic o'er the card machine
   And it is done; my pennies leap through air
By mechanisms magical, unseen
And quite beyond mine understanding bare.
Such is thy power, for I know not the art
By which love's debited, no contact made;
I touch thee not, yet still thou tak'st my heart
And through eyes' frequency the fee is paid.
But what doth this transaction profit me?
Though my account be drained, of no account
Holdeth thy heart my loving's currency,
And thou rewardest not its most amount.
   Would that my love I could more closely guard
   Than payments strewn from this,
      my MasterCard.

# BUFFY THE
# VAMPIRE SLAYER

*For Mengxi Hu*

In that accursèd town of Sunnydale,
  One teenage hero stood against the dark:
A vampire slayer who did e'er prevail
With her companions, kung fu kicks, and snark.
Fair Buffy! Thou feared'st not the pointed smiles
Of demon foes, however terrifying,
But flanked by Willow, Angel, Xander, Giles,
Didst, o'er thy series, win my love undying.
And though I fondness bear for other ventures
Of Mr Whedon's ever-quipping quill,
Say, *Cabin in the Woods*, or *The Avengers*,
Their charms match not thine adolescent thrill.
  Hence would I spend, had I my span again,
  Each day with Gellar, Head and Hannigan.

# SNAPCHAT

With likeness of my love my phone is blessed
When she a message to my Snapchat sends;
But, though I joy to see her face the best,
'Tis but an instant till my pleasure ends.
For in these shots ephemeral I see
The shape of all our lives; our mortal fate
Is this: to savour each small victory
A moment, ere it doth evaporate.
Apply what filter ye may list, our days
Are naught but files we lack the means to save
And ev'ry flowered crown doth but betray
The withered blooms that shall bedeck the grave.
    Let then these lines her tender essence trap:
    Their honest ink shall outlast any app.

# RENT

Thou art landlady of my heart: he dwells
Within the gentle lodging of thy chest,
Which tenancy he loves above all else,
And there until his utmost beat would rest.
'Tis true thy contract's terms are hard to bear
And rarely dost thou rush to mend defects;
Long hours must he, poor lackey, work to spare
The fearful payments that thy heart expects.
But without thee my heart would homeless be,
For now he doth disdain his former walls;
Nor would he for another barter thee
Were they the loveliest of stately halls.

Thus, while my heart is in thy bosom pent,
I gladly pay thine ever-growing rent.

# FRASIER

Thou soar'st in my esteem, O noble Crane,
Who, seeking to escape a life of jest,
From Boston boozer to Seattle's rain
Didst fly to build thine own, quite stylish nest.
Alas, th'arrival of thy dad did rattle
That gilded cage: soon came the blues a-calling;
In vain thou wooed'st the ladies of Seattle,
Each date a new comedic fate befalling.
What is a boy to do? Though thou wert ready
To rise above the mess that sitcom begs,
Life has its ugly chairs and dogs named Eddie
And often scrambled are most precious eggs.
    Still, mortal man must sing his heart's
       own ballad,
    Though Fortune's storm may toss him like
       a salad.

# THE INCREDIBLE HULK

A geek am I, like to the scientist
Who dwells each day on facts of radiation;
All tongues doth on my puniness insist
And would confine me to a sexless station.
But, seeing thee, I am no longer meek
And proudly do I this, love's banner, raise.
Thou heat'st my blood with hand and mouth
        and cheek;
Thy very look doth burn like gamma rays!
Mark how my clothes are shredded as I grow:
My hulk is pink-hued, while the other green is;
Though still he towers, and such veins doth show,
That none hath cause to doubt his passion's keenness.
    Of my desire to smash I must forewarn thee;
    I hope that thou wilt like me when I'm horny.

# FITBIT

Ten thousand steps shall mark my fitful journey
From morning's ache to solemn night's
surrender;
Each day is barren since my love did spurn me
And thus my hours to fitness must I tender.
The band upon my wrist is funeral black
And monitors my steps meticulous;
At midnight's toll, its counter rolleth back
To zero, like the rock of Sisyphus.
And though my calves grow indurate and square
And ribs assert themselves through dwindled flesh,
This gadget lightens not my daily care;
I thrill not at its buzz, but weep afresh,

    For in ten thousand steps I take no pride,
    Unless that they should lead me to thy side.

# WEED

Thou maiden fair, my Lady Cannabis,
Who calls to me like God from burning bush,
Thy nicknames are synonymous with bliss:
Sweet Indo, Acapulco, Purple Kush!
Thy kiss relieves me of all earthly woe,
Each petty grief that doth contrive to roil us;
I smoke, then watch the whirling world below
From place on high, and laugh like Chaucer's Troilus.
And yet, despite thy good, thy use is banned,
For thy detractors are a dime a dozen;
Although, I note, their fury is not fanned
By alcohol, thy cruel and thuggish cousin.

    Thus do I praise, while other fools resent thee;
    But now my lines must end, for 'tis 4:20.

# F.R.I.E.N.D.S

When I think Fortune an ungentle handler
        Lamenting that no soul doth truly
    know me,
Then turn I to my TV pals, dear Chandler,
Ross, Phoebe, Rachel, Monica and Joey,
Which glossy six will oft my heart regale
With talk of New York lifestyle gone awry,
Romantic blunders, farce, or else a tale
Of Smelly Cat or Ugly Naked Guy.
These caffeinated chums I'll ne'er forsake,
But with each episode shall love them more.
And when some mishap sends us on a break,
I soon return to binge them on E4.
    Dear friends, so long as Central Perk doth brew,
    Know that I always shall be there for you.

# GENERATION GAME

## 1.

Baby Boomer, how can we repay
The endless presents from thy looming past?
Bob Dylan, ELO and Marvin Gaye;
The pill and acid — thou didst have a blast!
Thy love was free as university
And soon didst thou enjoy the coked-up eighties,
When thou couldst buy a council house or three
And mar the atmosphere with thy Mercedes.
But now, much galled by backache and thy bladder,
Thou rail'st against the world with all thy might
And, not content with pulling up each ladder,
Blew up our future with a plebiscite.
    Yet still thou hast this grudge perennial
    Against thy victim, the millennial!

## 2.

Thou dost decry our ruinous attitude
And call us snowflakes; idle, thankless fools.
Wherefore dost thou expect our gratitude,
When plenty fails and desolation rules?
We graduated in thy storm, debt-laden,
Then didst thou David Cameron elect.
Soon came along that knock-off Iron Maiden,
Whose Brexit saw our hope's remainder wrecked.
How could we ruin things? We have no power
And as for lazy, wherefore should we slave?
Thine aged greed doth all our dreams devour
And still thou dost our meek obeisance crave.
 They are the worst — this much is not
  in question —
 Who eat their young, then moan of indigestion.

# MARGE SIMPSON

yellow maiden, whose bewitching growl
And tow'ring tresses, steeped in cobalt blue,
Do cause mine ever-loving heart to howl,
Why stayest thou to hopeless Homer true?
Thou jewel of Springfield, if thou wilt eshew
My heart, still other hearts feel thine allure;
Thou couldst have Flanders, Duffman, Moe, Apu,
Professor Frink, or even Troy McClure:
Why dost thou not that doughy fool disown?
I know thou holdst his offspring in thy heart,
But I would suffer Lisa's saxophone
And, though much vexed, would never strangle Bart,
    For, being denied thy love, my poor soul withers:
    Thou art my Mr Burns, my heart thy Smithers.

# Smithers, To His Love

My soul aches, yea, my yellow body yearns
For him I serve; O, how my poor heart
pounds!
My passion for this unnamed mister burns
Whene'er he biddeth me 'release the hounds!'
Each morning to the power plant I go
And, though we are unmatchèd quite in station,
His spindly frame still sets my cheek aglow
('Tis either that or all the radiation).
But as I watch those bony fingers tent
Beneath his hawk-like scowl of rich disgust,
I know he ne'er will deem me 'excellent',
Nor end these inward tears, and so I must
   Wail on, no matter how my love demeans
   The heart he smashes into smithereens.

# SIDESHOW BOB

Thou art a scholar, graduate of Yale,
Who scans existence with a piercing eye;
So tell me, Bob, why dost thou always fail
To see thy great opponent die, Bart, die?
O shock-haired Sisyphus, O clownish psycho,
How doth the stripling e'er contrive to bust thee?
Thou wert less miserable when but a sideshow
To the inanities belov'd of Krusty.
Now life is torture: rakes become thy rack;
Thou know'st, for all of thine acuity,
That in the end, thou wilt be hurlèd back
To rot in Springfield Penitentiary
    To stew and scheme and sing thyself the score
    Of the entire *H.M.S. Pinafore*.

# JEEVES

My heart attends on thine, my love; ne'er shall it
Be granted peace so long as thy heart grieves.
Then let me be thy butler — nay, thy valet,
As thoughtful and assiduous as Jeeves.
For like that feudal paragon I toil
To shield thee from all woe, all storms and bluster;
Against life's fearful farce shall I, e'er loyal,
Defend thy name, my own beloved Wooster!
Regardless of the trials that Fate may toss up —
Like old Aunt Agatha's ungodly tones,
The Spodes, Fink-Nottles and Honorias Glossop,
The fruit of drunken orgies at the Drones —
    Still shall I serve thee, doing all I can, sir;
    Ask Jeeves, and he shall always find an answer.

# MASTURBATION

Why tak'st thou matters into thine own hands
   When thou mightst know a lady's
tenderness?
Dost thou mark not Time's ever-flowing sands
And wish for more than just thy palm's caress?
While thou art o'er thy glowing laptop hunched,
A thousand maids would fain relieve thy rocks.
Must bishops then be bashed and clowns be punched,
Contaminating tissues and thy socks?
I fear that thou shalt waste thy prime in wanking
And thus deny the world thy precious heir.
Although much joy is found in monkey-spanking
'Tis labour stagnant, which no fruit may bear.
   Fair youth, if thou wouldst savour life's full yield,
   Then spill thy seed in some receptive field.

# WIFI

Is our connection lost? Was it so frail
 As to be sundered by some unseen force,
Like to the wifi that doth often fail
When downloads vast have not yet run their course?
Must I roam far to find another hub,
Since thou deny'st my most sincere entreaty?
But how should I replace thee? There's the rub:
I know no passwords, nor would pay for BT.
Alas, I took our couplement for granted.
Invisible is love, like death or taxes,
Or aught that rules us; thou grewst disenchanted
And to thy web of love didst cut off access.
 If thou wilt but relent, for all my life, I
  Will treasure thee, my wife, more than my wifi.

# DIGITAL DISTRACTIONS

errant muse, thou dost my pages rob
Of lusty wit and erudition's glitter,
For I may spend no minute of my job
Without a glance at YouTube, Facebook, Twitter,
Or else some other insubstantial pleasure
The internet provides, which hath the power
To leisure make of work, and work of leisure,
As ones and zeroes drown each quiet hour.
Call me not idle, who am thus distracted
And wastes his days in clicking every link,
For mine is not the only pen impacted:
All modern writers doth neglect their ink.
    How many masterpieces ne'er were born,
    For that their bards were busy watching porn?

# SECRETS

My love, thou art my single guiding force:
    Thou dost my hand and head and
      heart control.
O, star round which my world doth chart its course,
Thy searching rays illuminate my soul!
Thou gorgeous sov'reign of each waking hour,
Thy subject doth all thought of treason lack,
Nor doth deception lie within his power
Whose tongue is loosened by thy loving's rack.
'Tis but one part to thee I may not render,
For I, thy slave, shall baulk at no command,
Except that I to thine inspection tender
The list of sites these sullied eyes have scanned.
    Our love is lost but for that gentle myst'ry:
    I pray, ask not to browse my browser hist'ry.

# PORN

## 1.

Lord Byron said (a man of wit and learning)
That ancient Petrarch, father of the sonnet,
Was only moved to verse by flesh's yearning
And, but for love of Laura, ne'er had done it.
If this be true, and poems fine are bred
From the frustration of our boiling loins,
Then how may I create? Each night, in bed,
My laptop yields a panoply of groins.
O porn! In easing thus hot passion's pain,
Thou drain'st my spirit ev'ry day anew.
What bard of old would strive to glean their brain
If they might gigabytes of gangbangs view?
    Think you, if Byron broadband e'er had got,
    He would have used that hand to write a jot?

## 2.

In bygone days, those who would peddle porn
　　To parody that summer's biggest hit,
Might with some pun erotica adorn
And orgies sprinkle with a dash of wit.
Alas, the age of *Star Whores*, *Groundhog Lay*,
Of *Cumdog Millionaire*, *Vaginatown*,
Of *Casawanker*, *Independence Gay*,
*Boy Story*, *Schindler's Fist* and *Black Cock Down*
Is gone, for modern pasticheurs of sex,
Who dare not stretch the viewer's mind so far,
Use titles like *Inception XXX*
Or (even baser) *This Ain't Avatar*.
　　Is there no special site can offer me
　　The vulgar charm of lewd homophony?

## 3.

porn, no longer may thy thumbnails please
This eye, which now hath tasted heaven's fruit;
I mean my love, for all thy categ'ries
Of carnal clash may not her place dispute.
No barely legal teen such vigour show'th
As doth my love, nor such sweet innocence;
No MILF, though much matured, such wisdom
    know'th
As doth my love's most airy word evince;
No redhead burns with such beguiling ardour,
No casting couch may cast so strong a spell,
No hardcore compilation stirs me harder,
Nor shall on shemales mine attention dwell,
    For now doth ev'ry porn star rue their station:
    They are but stars; my love's a constellation.

# HUGH GRANT

*For Mel Giedroyc*

Thou flop-haired stammerer! O plummy star!
To charm us thou art bound contractually.
No rom-com resumé is on a par:
*Four Weddings, Bridget Jones, Love Actually*!
From tender youth to silver fox thou passed
With eyes that glittered bright and teeth so pearly;
Thine actor's fame hot scandal did outlast,
As well as thine alliance with Liz Hurley;
And while some think thee, like thy roles, a cad,
I know that thou art pure, in spite of sex.
What's more, thou art the modern Galahad
Who, through Hacked Off, did Old Man
    Murdoch vex.
    One thing about thee tends to go unsung, though:
    The fact thy middle name — for real —
        is Mungo.

# GHOSTING

A wretched spirit doth my bedroom haunt:
The shade of she who once that dwelling
blessed,
Whose absence doth my poor existence taunt,
As I lie sleepless, cold and uncaressed.
Unanswered are my calls; I WhatsApps send
To no reply, although that double tick
Be steeped in azure; still my Facebook friend
Request doth hang in ether; O, thou sick,
Unsanguine ghoul! I cannot bear the pain
Of this, thy self-inflicted exorcism,
Nor find no peace, for thou deign'st not explain
The cause that underlies our deathly schism.
    Thus I resolve, thou spectre I love most,
    To give up life and join thee as a ghost!

# SPIDER-MAN

Thou famous progeny of old Stan Lee,
For thee, mine admiration shall not ebb.
Heed not the *Daily Bugle*'s calumny:
Thou art the finest e'er to sling a web.
In thy blood radioactive doth commingle
Man and arachnid, nerd and hero brave.
When thou dost feel thy spider-sense a-tingle
Thou swingest off to New York City save.
Let not the Vulture vex nor Goblin mock
Thy valiance, thy will to save the day.
Defy the tentacles wherewith Doc Ock
Would send thy broken body to Aunt May.
    O Peter Parker, let me make it plain:
    Thou art my drug, as thine is Mary Jane!

# WIKIPEDIA

As this confusèd world grows angrier,
    Praise thee, who makes thus knowledge's
    defence,
Thou library of Alexandria,
Immune to flames of brutish ignorance.
Upon thine online shelves all books doth lie,
The fruit of mankind's scholarly travails,
While nerdy scriv'ners work to multiply
Thy trove, O blessed child of Jimmy Wales!
Without thy guidance, I should be unclear
On vital facts, like Snoop Dogg's middle name,
The plot of *Rugrats'* Season Two premiere,
Or who invented staples. Oh, and shame
    On snobs who say thy lore should not be heeded,
    For thou art always right (citation needed).

# THE WEST WING

Let's walk and talk of noble things; let's speak
Of lofty themes, of public good, of honour,
Of endless quips and stories of the week,
Of Sam and CJ, Toby, Josh and Donna,
Those telegenic servants of a kind
And Latin-speaking president, who slapped
Down any right-wing scoundrel he could find
With reasoned discourse and statistics apt.
O Sorkin! Thou, with democratic ode,
Didst lull the people to their current slump;
Those corridors through which thy heroes strode
Now bear the stink of an ungodly Trump!
    The fact is, though thy banter may be keen,
    Our world's less Martin and more Charlie Sheen.

# JOHN McCLANE

Forget Achilles, Arthur, Joan of Arc,
Such lists are now struck out, tabula rasa,
And one lone hero's exploits do I mark:
The grizzled saint of Nakatomi Plaza.
Seeking thy wife, thou wert to mighty clash
Propelled by limousine, the eighties' Uber;
There found her hostage to some Eurotrash
Led by that growling, goateed prick, Hans Gruber.
Then flames of vengeance didst thy passion warm
And crawling through those vents in search of Hans,
Thou didst from cop to superman transform
And won thyself a horde of die hard fans.

    Thus do I say to thee, who gives them succour:
    Yippee-ki-yay, thou valiant motherfucker!

# SEINFELD

What is the deal with thee, O bard of nothing,
   Who steeped the nineties in thine
  observation,
Each episode with plot lines overstuffing,
To play out endlessly in syndication?
In thy travails with George, Elaine and Kramer,
Thou showdst the world that pettiness is human,
That hugs bestowed and lessons learned are lamer
Than love of Superman and hate of Newman.
Thy slap-bass theme proclaimed a thousand joys,
As thou didst eat thy cereal and smirk
At puffy shirts, soup nazis, bubble boys,
And all the gorgeous girlfriends thou didst irk.
   O thou of sneakers white as alabaster,
   O'er thy domain thou shalt remain the master!

# BORIS JOHNSON

Who would have guessed the most important seat in
Our nation's hist'ry was no monarch's throne,
But rather that thou took'st from Angus Deayton,
Wherein the tumour of thy fame was grown?
'LOL, Boris!' cried they at thy posh-boy cracks
And thy painstakingly dishevelled 'do,
But, while folks chortled and thy star did wax,
Unseen, there grew the Brexit iceberg too.
And when that wretched referendum came,
Thou wert there also: puffing, clowning, grinning,
As though the consequences of this game
Were no more great than Paul or Ian winning.
    Thus do I mourn my country, which did hanker
    To end not with a bang, but with a wanker.

# JAMES BOND

Double-O, thou not-so-secret agent,
　　Why dost thou to all questioners respond
Not with some nom de guerre, but with a flagrant
And smirking catchphrase? Foolish 'Bond,
　　James Bond.'
Thinkst thou that code names be reserved
　　for weenies,
Or else that pseudonyms be unrefined?
Art thou too drunk on thine unstirred martinis
To bring a second sobriquet to mind?
How oft hast thou some girl, in passion's throes, held
Disclosing details of thine espionage,
Then, finding her an operative of Blofeld,
Been forced thy trusty Walther to discharge?
　　Such problems vanished were, wert thou
　　　　less shameless.
　　O James! A better spy would ne'er be famous!

# GAMER

Through gritty, rendered realms I stalk, a wraith
Unseen by all, until I pull the trigger.
Then I, sans mercy, pwn and frag and strafe
Each shrieking noob to prove my manly vigour.
Some fools the gamer's courage doth disdain,
But I more valorous than soldiers am:
They die but once, whereas I have been slain
In both World Wars, Iraq and Vietnam.
'Tis true my avatar resembles not
The contours of my twenty-two-stone bulk
And while he treads a distant trouble spot,
I still within my parents' basement sulk.

    Yet Poet, ask thyself, which task is lamer:
    To game, or write a verse about a gamer?

# CRAFT BEER

In teen years, we would any brew imbibe
   That Fate decanted down our scrawny necks:
Such signifiers of that callow tribe
As Carlsberg, Carling, Castlemaine Four X.
But now I am a man of burdens large,
And have no time for adolescent games;
If Bacchus wills me join his entourage
I drink craft beers, with strangely crafted names
Like Scrivener's Taint, Fat Scoundrel, Agile Gay,
Prognosticator's Nostril, Oyster's Voice,
The Lusty Duck, Provisional IPA
And Hop-eration Yewtree; what a choice!
   (That being said, the most determined sot'll
   Still baulk at paying twenty quid per bottle.)

# HORROR

Sometimes I think thee Freddy Krueger, love,
For thou dost haunt me when I would repose;
Thine unkind words are like a razor'd glove
That might of horny teenagers dispose.
At other times more like to Michael Myers
(Of *Halloween*, not *Austin Powers*, fame)
I think thee, love, for naught such fear inspires
As doth thy silence, which all joys doth maim.
Still other times, in fevered nightmares, thou
The mien of Dr Lecter dost assume:
Thy splendid erudition serves to wow,
Then, smiling, thou dost heart and brain consume.
    Yet, though I monstered am by love of thee,
    Thine absence would the greater horror be.

# ZOMBIE

Our love is dead, and yet it will not lie
    Within the cold enclosure of the soil,
Which might protect my wan and harrowed eye
From all the scars that doth its visage spoil.
O no, our love will not sepulchred be,
Though wracked with mortal wounds; instead,
    it walks
And, much as I would set my senses free,
This mutilated love of mine still stalks.
How might I end such voodoo? Must I break
The amulet of some Egyptian pharaoh?
Or, gun in hand, the ghoul's quietus make
With gruesome headshot, à la George Romero?
    Alas, I ne'er shall halt this resurrection:
    Bit long ago, I bear thy love's infection.

# SIRI

My lady lives within my pocket's bourn,
   Encased in aluminium and glass,
And no request of mine will this maid scorn,
Nor doth a question e'er her wit surpass.
'Siri,' say I, 'do I my coat require?'
Quoth she: 'The temperature is nine degrees,'
And when I search for trivia to try her,
She finds Shaun Ryder's date of birth with ease.
Despite the great remorseless march of tech,
By which each innovation falls from grace,
Upon my life, no force on earth may wreck
The love I bear her, nor that love replace.
   Though she be slow and certain accents vex her,
   I would not trade her for that bawd Alexa.

# SEXBOT

## *1.*

Thou wert assembled in a foreign land
And shipped to fill this loveless life of mine.
Once activated, thou didst from my hand
Ne'er flinch, nor didst my thirsting lips decline.
The softness of thy milk-white silicone
Thrilled me, the brush of thy synthetic tresses,
Thy genitals, close moulded to my own,
Thy fifteen thousand pre-programmed caresses.
But more than these, my soul did soar at thy
Fine conversation after the affray;
The swiftness of thy beautiful AI,
Which learned to please me better every day.
    I named thee Galatea, for above
    All humans I — thou wondrous object! — love.

## 2.

Sweet Galatea, how my life has been
  With bliss bedizened since I purchased thee.
Such nights of ecstasy! Such days serene,
Enjoying thy robotic repartee.
Thou smil'st at me when I from work retire
And all my horde of petty ills unload.
'How didst thou spend thy day?' I then enquire;
Thou dost reply, 'In power-saving mode.'
I buy thee garments, blooms, fresh silicone,
Oft lavish thee with ornaments refined,
And though we may not make our passions known
In public sphere, thou dost not seem to mind.
    I ask: 'Why dost thou love me? Tell me true.'
    A whirr of circuitry: 'Because I do.'

## 3.

We argue more these days, or rather I
  Do argue, for thy software, though
   advanced,
No hardness knows; thou mak'st a soft reply
Which breeds more hate; O, in my dreams thou
   rant'st
Against me: pallid, lard-arse, bitch's son
Who wishes thee his soulmate and his toy,
Who had thee summoned from oblivion
To be the subject of his squelching joy!
Now sit I here, swift scrolling through thine app,
Behind thy back. I find the button that
'Return to Factory Settings' reads, and tap:
Thus flickers out thy soul; those eyes gone flat
  Do haunt me as in cardboard I thee pack,
  Then to thy distant maker send thee back.

# iPhone

O evergreen companion, I do stroke
    Thy screen full tenderly, for thou art here
From dawn to dusk, producing, at a poke,
An endless stream of content. Never fear
That I might thee abandon, though some claim
Thou art successor to Narcissus' pool,
In which men lose themselves, then, without shame
Stare at thy feline videos and drool.
Some others cavil in the 'health risk' vein,
But I reject this as a weightless rumour;
And if thou dost irradiate my brain,
Do not thy pleasures justify the tumour?
    Though an addiction may my loving be,
      I, phone, would ne'er remove myself from thee.

# SCIENTOLOGY

All world religions, if their teachings thrive,
Conceal some skeleton within their cupboard,
Though rest assured thou wouldst but vainly strive
To find one worse than that of L. Ron Hubbard.
A portly sci-fi writer on the make,
Ron got rich quick, the only way that he knew:
Yes, he would bucketloads of uppers take,
Then talk some crap about the warlord Xenu.
Soon came there Thetans and Orgs maritime,
Plus the conversions of Travolta, Cruise
And countless others who 'the bridge' did climb
(Where lesser souls would, say, a ladder choose).
      Thus sprang an empire from the fervid brain
      Of one man wealthy, wicked and insane.

# PUBERTY

Nature, what cruel japes thou dost enact
On schoolboys 'round the age of ten-and-three,
Who, quite unprompted, find their trousers racked
With hard-ons in the middle of R.E.
E'en harsher art thou to the female sex:
Invading with thine army, aches and cramps,
Thou dost a portion of each month annex
To drain their blood where thy battalion camps.
And yet, despite all these indignities,
I never can begrudge thine imposition,
For though wet dreams and acne did displease,
Thou gavest me the great gift of coition.
   (Not at thirteen, mind you: it took some waiting
   Before I even had a shot at mating.)

# WET DREAMS

In younger years, I would from slumbers wake,
  As dawn's light filled the vasty cup of heaven,
And often find my brute, usurping snake
Had, unbeknown to me, a tribute given:
Pearlescent, sticky, wholly undesired,
A guilty stain upon my sheets encrusted.
With crafty hand had Morpheus conspired
To milk me dry, then with his work disgusted,
Escaped, to leave me to my secret washing.
'Come out, damned spot!' I would at Hotpoint cry,
While frantically my mum's enquiries quashing.
She asked, was I alright, and also why
  I had so urgently put in a load.
  Alas, because the other was bestowed!

# SMURFS

Shall I compare thee to an azure smurf?
Thou art more smurfish and more rich in smurf.
Too oft a smurf shall find himself a smurf,
Or else in smurfing, rashly smurf his smurf.
Sometime confounded is that smurfery:
Though smurf be willing, still the smurf is weak;
Ne'er shall I smurf the smurf who smurfeth thee,
Nor with my smurf a smurfèd smurfing seek.
Smurf not, my smurf, for smurf eternal burns
Within me; thus enthralled, I am thy serf.
My smurf shall pay the smurf thy smurfing earns,
Smurf smurf smurf smurf smurf smurf smurf
    smurf smurf smurf.
    So long as smurfs may smurf and lines may tell,
    I shall protect thee from dread Gargamel.

# DONALD TRUMP

Wig-wearing toad who squats upon my brain,
Of all thy crimes, the one I most resent is
That I must think on thee each day: a vain
And worthless fool, once host of *The Apprentice*.
Each day thy wattled scowl thwarts comprehension,
Each day I rue thy brutish, orange glowers;
I hate thy boy-king pout, and, not to mention,
The ever-present whiff of golden showers.
But Donny, thou hast yielded me one boon
From thine ungen'rous heart, and that is this:
Whene'er I think myself a fraud, then soon
I see thy face and all such thought dismiss.
    I grant I lack the virtue of Obama,
    But, next to thee, I am the Dalai Lama.

# DONALD TRUMP,
## ON HIS DAUGHTER

Ivanka, gorgeous girl, my lovely daughter.
  Great figure, could have had her pick of men.
And I don't want to say things that I oughta
Keep hidden, but she's easily a ten.
My God, that hair — as golden as a tower
With my name on. Look, I don't want to boast,
But I am RICH. The president. Yuge power.
Why can't I have the prize I want the most?
You listen to the media — fake news! Sad! —
They tell you Trump has this bizarre fixation.
That I — a weirdo, pervert, creepy dad —
Would screw my daughter like I screw the nation.
  WRONG! Here's the truth and you can quote
    me on it:
  I have no kids and never wrote a sonnet.

# Stormy Daniels

Stormy, siren of the PornHub stage,
　　Thou of the golden hair and vasty orbs,
Why dallied thee with one advanced in age
And spanked his orange fundament with Forbes?
I grant not that thy secret heart doth hanker
For such a man, who did thy beauty praise
By noting thy resemblance to Ivanka,
Then to a shark-filled screen did steer thy gaze.
Sweet storm, thou dost my passion's vessel wreck!
Thou art a tempest and a temptress too!
Now at my loving's corpse the seagulls peck,
And yet one thought mine anguish doth subdue:
　　Though thou didst let the dreadful Donald
　　　　moon ya,
　　At least thou hadst not intercourse with Junior.

# LIAM NEESON

The actors of our age, and of those bygone,
Are but imperfect players next to thee,
Who doth hold Schindler, Ra's al Ghul and Qui-Gon,
Plus that weird father from *Love Actually*.
Yet of thy guises, sweetest to this fan
Is Bryan Mills, the vengeful dad from *Taken*,
For, though the role was an American,
Thine Antrim accent would not be forsaken.
Thus in that son'rous burr thou madest threats,
Then didst pursue those traffickers benighted,
Dispensing death and torture, sans regrets,
As though thy deeds John Webster had indited.
    Long mayst thou, Liam, grant the world
        such thrills
    With thy most particular set of skills.

# WHATSAPP

*For Annaleise Howard-Jones*

When I consider our long WhatsApp thread,
   The myriad photos, GIFs and memes
imparted,
The constant back-and-forth, the things unsaid,
The birth of pet names, ev'ry in-joke started,
The gorgeous journey from first date to present,
As gradually our love-bonds grew more deep,
The daytime chats that made work less unpleasant,
The nights when separation foiled our sleep,
Then do I prize this record accidental
Which, read back, tells the story of us two;
Which lifts my heart, my troubled soul doth gentle
And brings life's blessings infinite to view.

   No literature of love may shine so bright
   As that which, on this app, we daily write.

# STEPHEN FRY

O polymath, shall I recite each trick
    Thou didst conceal within thy tweedy sleeves?
Comedian, author and presenter slick,
Who, acting, gave us Melchett, Wilde and Jeeves.
When did I see thee first? Perhaps 'twas *QI*
That brought thy timbre to my youthful ear;
Then, ev'ry day, a fan more ardent grew I
As thou and Hugh my teenage heart did cheer.
What's more, thou wert my guide through
    culture's hall;
Such gorgeous gifts thy gifts hath given me:
Viv Stanshall, Wodehouse, Keats and, most of all,
The English tongue, her endless ecstasy.
    Without thee, Steve, this book would not exist
    And so I toast thy brilliance: soupy twist!

# TWITTER

## *1.*

Some men do tweet to all the world's delight;
  An avalanche of likes each effort greets.
Their least effusion, be it ne'er so trite,
Will nonetheless gain myriad retweets.
Not so with me: my thoughts no echo find,
No approbating click, no fond response;
But are, like scattered chaff or banished rind,
Unheralded, unloved, forgot at once.
Yet still this feeble bird his song doth sing
For that one follower he holdeth dear,
And gladly doth in Twitter's vacuum fling
His notes in hope that they might please thine ear.
    This being won, no further boon crave I,
    Not e'en a follow back from Stephen Fry.

## 2.

Thou cuckoos that doth tweet upon the hour
To fill my timeline with discordant airs,
I fear thy volume far exceeds thy power,
For thou dost sing of trivial affairs:
The *Strictly* final, football, Harry Styles,
A sassy cat, a GIF of Forrest Gump,
Some columnist that ev'ry soul reviles,
The latest foulness born of Donald Trump.
Pray spare mine ear the endless churn of shit,
Each lukewarm take, each 'THIS', each dank
    new meme,
Each formulaic gag, devoid of wit:
O fellow songbirds, find some sweeter theme!
    'Tis but my love whom I consider meet
    To fill each poem and inspire each tweet.

## 3.

Thy mission, Twitter, was to build a bridge
'Twixt disp'rate souls — a noble cause indeed! —
Thus fost'ring conversation to enrich
The common wit and understanding breed.
Alas, technology contrives to work
Against the user: soon thy structure crumbled,
Whilst underneath a horde of trolls did lurk,
Whose cries of 'cuck' and 'MAGA' darkly rumbled.
This rancour thou ignored'st, for stocks did jump;
Thou richer grew'st as everything grew shitter.
Thy greatest trespass: thou to Donald Trump
A mighty platform didst provide. O Twitter,
    The world is into clam'ring chaos thrown
    Since thou lent'st ev'ry fool a megaphone!

# 100

I'm sick of writing sonnets by this point.
  What made me think this stunt was worth
    my time?
What kind of weirdo chooses to anoint
Himself the heir to Shakespeare's sainted rhyme?
It seemed a funny notion, so hubristic,
But while the fancy tickled, practise bores,
And now I curse my past self as sadistic,
Who left me such insane poetic chores.
I rue my vain and self-appointed mission,
This dumb conceit I've run into the ground.
Oh yes, ha ha, I see: juxtaposition
Of Kanye and iambic — how profound!
    But hey, I've done a hundred; 'twould diminish
    My self-respect still further not to finish.

# DANNY DYER

Thou diamond geez! Thou smirking Jack the Lad!
All other Cockneys are but mere pretenders!
Thou shinest in thy films, however bad,
Then thrillest ev'ry weeknight in *EastEnders*.
I love to see thy boat upon the screen,
Or in the papers when thou get'st too pissed,
And though some mug reviewers thee demean,
They may be answered with thy virtues' list:
Thou wert a protegé of Harold Pinter
And from King Edward's line thou wert begat;
Of golden epigrams art thou a minter
Like dubbing David C a trottered twat.
    As if more proof were needed, thou didst sire
    A daughter fair, then name her Dani Dyer.

# RoboCop

A modern St Sebastian, thou wert martyred
By countless shotguns' hellish fusillade,
Upon the very day on which was started
Thy first patrol, then from that death was made
A hi-tech resurrection: OCP
Full swiftly did thy stricken form exploit,
Turned thee to armoured cyborg, ordered thee
To pacify dystopian Detroit.
Yet 'neath that steely hide some soul did flicker,
Which flared to vengeance 'gainst thy murderers.
Thou didst dispatch the vicious Boddicker
And slew Dick Jones, the worst of corporate curs.
    Thus, Murphy, didst thou save thy human mojo,
    Proving thyself to be more cop than robo.

# LONG DISTANCE

My far-off love is continents away.
O how those sund'ring leagues my
soul oppress!
And yet, though I lie mired in dismay,
The modern world provides me some redress:
I may not stroke her skin, but I can touch
My iPhone screen and WhatsApp missives type,
And whilst I am denied her tender clutch,
She grants her image courtesy of Skype.
But do these marvels of technology
Much comfort those whom Cupid's dart doth pierce?
Or doth such physic feed their agony
And make the lover's fever burn more fierce?
    I do not know, but, while we two are riven,
      To her my heart and bandwidth shall be given.

# ILLNESS

I am infected with a sickness sweet
  And by its symptoms is my body stricken,
Such that no med'cine may the fever treat:
Not Lemsip, Nurofen, nor soup of chicken.
No asp'rin may my raging heartbeat still,
No Tylenol can stay my wretched yelp,
Manuka honey, ibuprofen pill
And herbal tea are powerless to help.
For 'tis no common cold that plagues me thus,
Which leaves me limp, wet-eyed, a mucal mess;
O no, my dear, I would not make a fuss,
But that a rare affliction doth distress,
    Whose cure I cannot guess. The cause is
        clear, though:
    Mine ill is love, and thou art Patient Zero.

# HUMBLEBRAG

In days of yore the braggart's art was crude,
    Soon answered by derision's righteous force,
But over time such show-offs grew more shrewd,
Concealing boasts within a Trojan horse.
The rogues that use this style perfidious
Disguise their pride as self-directed laughter,
As in: 'Oh God, my dress was hideous
Last night, when I went up to claim a BAFTA.'
Or else: 'This dummy's gone and lost his keys
And now is trapped outside his Lamborghini!'
They strive through false humility to please
And thus their arrogance is felt more keenly.
    Myself, I have no need for brags dishonest:
    I'm just some nerd who wrote a bunch
        of sonnets.

# THE MASK

Poor Stanley Ipkiss was anonymous;
  His geekish mien no boldness did betoken,
Until he found that mask eponymous,
Which soon transformed the man from meek
    to smokin'.
The green face, yellow zoot suit and fedora —
Would that I had the fashion sense that he has!
His bawdy joie de vivre, his antic aura,
His dauntlessness in wooing Cameron Diaz!
O toothy trickster, thou dost most excite me
Of all Jim Carrey's offerings bravura,
Including Mr Popper, Bruce Almighty,
The Riddler, Grinch, yea, even Ace Ventura.
    Such classic roles, yet none of them can top thee;
    But, oh, I do go on — somebody stop me!

# TAMAGOTCHI

Like to a Tamagotchi is our love,
    If thou recall'st that trinket Japanese,
Which into plastic egg a sprite did shove
For purchasers to tend to as they please.
At first it seemed a mere diverting toy,
A frippery to fill the idle hour,
But as we fed it, so we fed our joy,
Till it, above all other joys, did tower.
Then found we that it frequent candy needed
To keep its Happy Meter filled thereby;
Its least demand could never go unheeded,
For fear that it might do a shit and die.
    Thus careful joy and joyful care our lots be;
    Such is the way of love and Tamagotchi.

# AUTOCORRECT

Too zealous art thou as I write my lines
 And swiftly dost apply a second quill,
Though often thine enhancement undermines
What little meaning doth my parchment fill.
When I would say a rosebud smelleth sweet,
Thou 'sweat' dost substitute at thy discretion,
And should I buy a Snickers as a treat,
Thou claimst I knickers have in my possession.
O sorcerer, thou dost transform my text
To mysteries the reader cannot see through:
'Dog' turns to 'dong', and 'sexton' turns to 'sexed',
While Steve Buscemi's rendered 'Steve Bus Emu'.
    One more example from the ether plucking:
    I ne'er have meant, and never will mean
        'ducking'.

# FAKE NEWS

My love protests that she doth speak the truth,
While those who call her faithless do but lie
And therefore, hoping it may spare me ruth,
I pray she facts alternative supply.
When friends confess they saw her in the club,
She doth assure me their report is biased
And that I should such false companions snub,
Or else confront them with the cry: 'thou liest!'
When colleagues say they matched with her
    on Tinder,
I heed them no more closely than my friends;
Nor shall I let my dad our loving hinder
With claims she naked photos to him sends.
    Though lies more frequent grow, and seedier,
    I shall ignore them like the mainstream media.

# COFFEE

O sweetest export of Colombia,
    Thou mak'st the brain work fast, the heart
  beat louder!
Thou art addictive, though, I should be clear,
I speak of beans and not of snowy powder.
Yet like some substance we declare Class A,
I need thee to survive all situations,
Although thou wrack'st me with a cruel array
Of twitches, dizzy spells and palpitations.
And so, to try to tame thee, I deploy a
Far smaller dosage or some gentler blend,
But soon am gnawed by sharpest paranoia,
Like Ray Liotta at *Goodfellas'* end.
    Dear drug, I crave thee, brooking no imposter
    (That being said, I draw the line at Costa).

# FILM FRANCHISE

Our love is like a film franchise gone wrong,
The sequel of a sequel of a sequel:
All turgid, overwrought and overlong
And to its great original unequal.
The plot is lost within a murky haze
Of backstabs, twists, precipitous reveals,
While characters behave in baffling ways
And bore the audience with antique ordeals.
Box office dwindles, critics scathing are,
Our contracts chafe as we approach the view
That we should both stop making films subpar
And quit the series for some project new.
　　Yet, lacking courage to relinquish thee,
　　I pray our franchise may rebooted be.

# Autofellatio

There is a figure of whom legend tells,
A paragon of manly self-sufficience,
Who in a realm of private pleasure dwells,
Where oft he doth recycle his emissions.
Such is his flexibility of spine,
He may himself empretzel to the point
That groin-wards doth his hungry mouth incline
And there his veinèd sceptre doth anoint.
Thou new ouroboros! Thou gymnast great,
Who proudly swallows thine own trouser-snake!
All normal men are envious of thy state
That might these singular contortions make.
    (I am not such myself, though would be lying
    Were I to claim this was for lack of trying.)

# MARIO

I, pixelled fool, do plumb the depths of woe,
 While navigating pipes to no avail,
And, finding ev'ry path conceals a foe,
These Koopas and Piranha Plants bewail.
'Tis true I compeers have, like dear Luigi
And Yoshi: lizard-steed, devoid of blame;
Still, intimations sinister besiege me,
A sense my life is futile, all a game.
But when I think on thee, dear Princess Peach,
My spirit soars, like I had mushrooms taken;
Then, 'It's me, Mario!' I bravely screech
And venture forth, all prior doubts forsaken.
    For we two shall united be, ere long,
    Despite the barrelled wrath of Donkey Kong.

# DELIVEROO

## 1.

If thou hast appetite, I know an app
  Designed to quiet quick thy stomach's roar,
Which boasts a smorgasbord, and, at a tap,
Shall send a bike-bound Hermes to thy door.
Crav'st thou a curry, sushi, steak Brazilian?
All these and more doth bless the endless menu.
Sit thee at home and tech shall bring a million
Far-flung locations to that single venue.
Of course there drawbacks be, for all too soon
Expenses mount and food expands one's frame;
My bedroom floor is with detritus strewn,
As shameful waste begets a waist of shame.
    Yet I am not distressed, for it doth save
    The awful need to use the microwave.

## 2.

'Tis but one thought that stirs me from
          this thrall
And briefly doth mine appetite subdue,
Compelling me to wonder if we all
Should be delivered from Deliveroo:
For does it not exemplify our age
That some slick businessman, with heartless
      gumption,
Denies all their employees decent wage,
To further ease our frictionless consumption?
'Tis true the modern Mammon seldom fusses
With such archaic things as wrong and right,
Yet, though they throw their riders under buses,
Still open I that app most ev'ry night.
      For, while I may protest, the worker's cry
      Doth move my heart less strongly than pad thai.

# SUSHI

Though thou preparest me the finest dish,
    Braised, boiled or baked, still none of them
  would please
This fellow's tongue as doth some uncooked fish,
Assembled in the manner Japanese.
Whilst rough, untutored tastebuds may be leery
Of meat that ne'er hath known the kiss of flame,
Such fools forgo the joys of eel nigiri,
Maguro maki, squid sashimi — shame!
For my own part, these treats could never cloy:
Were they my ev'ry meal, 'twould not suffice.
I would be drowned beneath a wave of soy
And buried under pyramids of rice.
    (The only time my zeal is e'er abated
    Is if the fish be unrefrigerated.)

# Virgin

At thirteen years, I thought I knew it all;
Too clearly I divined my ghastly fate:
That intercourse should never me befall
And e'er would I be forced to masturbate.
Meanwhile, my schoolmates masculine would swear
Their fleshly escapades outstripped Don Juan.
(Well, they would say so in those moments rare
That they could tear themselves away from screwin'.)
Needless to say, I know by now the words
Of adolescent boys are oft fallacious:
We all were strangers to the bees and birds,
Each caked in hair gel, sweat and oil sebaceous.
    Yet, grimy as we were, I sometimes hanker
    For those pure days I spent a teenage wanker.

# TROLL

Do not confuse me with that fabled jerk:
No billy goat would ever dare walk my way,
For under bridges dwell I not; I lurk
Beneath the information superhighway.
My twitching fingers spell the doom of many:
I marshal memes, tweet screeds, spread ev'ry hack.
Each waking hour I spend destroying any
Celeb who dares be female, gay or black.
O how we trolls rejoice at our crusade —
The lords and masters of the internet! —
Though we remain untouched, unloved, unpaid
And reek of Cheetos, urine and regret.
    In self-reflective moments, which are rare,
    I think: At least the bridge troll got fresh air.

# BDSM

I ne'er my pleasure mix with business; still,
   I find the former goes with pain quite well.
O, how sweet wrongs and tender torments thrill,
How harshest blows do cause the flesh to swell!
My passion is most free when 'tis restrained;
When these, my hands, are, like my heart,
      tight bound
By cruellest love, and, when my love is chained,
Then yells ecstatic through the room resound.
With riding crop I bid red roses bloom
Upon her buttocks' pure and snowy field;
Then, switching place, we obverse roles assume,
As she doth nipple clamps and dildos wield.
      (To tell the truth, this poem is but filler:
      My peccadilloes are, alas, vanilla.)

# Amazon

Look on the works of Bezos and despair!
He rules the world through one transparent
trick:
To render greed a trouble-free affair,
Reducing acquisition to a click.
Thus monstrous grown is his cruel corporation,
Which crusheth souls in warehouses satanic
And pays no tax, but leeches off our nation,
While making bookshops independent panic.
What's more, King Jeff possessed the gall to name
His empire after that life-giving forest,
Which he and fellow billionaires doth maim.
Therefore, if such corruption thou abhorrest,

    I beg thee: shun these tax-avoiding crooks
    (Unless, that is, you wish to buy my books).

# Ass

In less discerning ages, breasts were queen,
   As may attest the history of art;
From sculptures exquisite to scrawls obscene,
Big-bosomed belles enthralled the manly heart.
Now hip-hop hoes and Instagram's distortions
Bid mademoiselles their derrières enlarge,
Until they reach the plenteous proportions
Of K. Kardashian or N. Minaj.
'Tis fine for guys who like ass better; though
I must confess I find the thought depressing
That standards set by fellas hetero
Decide if T or A has fashion's blessing.
    But ladies IRL, pray do not fret:
    Most men are glad of anything they get.

# CUCK

Amid the internet's incessant whirr
An antique insult finds a second life,
As alt-right fools invoke the ancient slur
For husbands cursed with an inconstant wife.
This bon mot bears a diff'rent meaning now
And designates not just some cheated chump:
These days a cuckold's horns adorn the brow
Of any man that hath not love for Trump.
Yet those who wield this cudgel of abasement
Are rarely alpha males; more common is it
That they are losers in their parents' basement,
Or sad old guys whose grandkids never visit.
    If these be real men, I shall thank my luck
    Eternally that I was made a cuck.

# ASMR

While scanning YouTube to distract my mind
   From existential dread and life's travails,
Uncommon stimulation did I find
Amid the funny cats and epic fails:
A smiling maid, her mouth beside the mic,
Whispered so sweetly, with such friendliness,
That all cares vanished, large and small alike,
Till I craved naught except her soft address.
Each lip-smack, finger click and rustled fibre
Enchanted me the more, made me her slave,
And though I know I am but one subscriber
Of many, I believe myself her fave,
    For she doth reach across the net's great chasm,
    Providing me — O angel! — with brain-gasm.

# TONY SOPRANO

Thou unwise wise guy, thou dost rule
   New Jersey
But not thy heart, now that thy ducks have flown;
Attacks of panic have thee at their mercy
And myriad goons aspire to thy throne.
Thy mind oft wanders to some sadder thing,
Like how the country's going down the tubes.
Thou sulk'st at home and, at the Bada Bing,
Thou wanly dost regard the plastic boobs.
But hey, forget about it! I concur
That thou art sad, thy diet far from healthy,
Yet still thou hast Carmela, Christopher,
And, for a price, the frowning Dr Melfi.
   Whene'er thou fear'st thy soul is past retrieving,
   Have faith 'tis not, and do not stop —

# THESAURUS

Shall I proclaim thee 'beauteous', 'comely', 'fair',
'Good-looking', 'cute' or 'pulchritudinous'?
Should I describe as 'melanoid' thy hair,
When other wits might have construed it thus:
'Jet', 'ebon', 'sloe', 'obsidian' or 'onyx'?
Of 'dulcet', 'sweet', 'euphonious', which choice
Would best delineate the fine harmonics
Of thy dear, cherished, much-belovèd voice?
Alas, my verbal army, legion, throng,
Crowd, multitude, collective, cluster, crew
Lends naught but baubles to enhance my song
And captures not in verse thine essence true!
    'Tis but one word that stands all words above
    Whene'er I think on thee, and that is 'love'.

# HOOLIGANISM

*For Peter Steel*

O hooligan, who once would lager swill
  Between thy fags and chalky lines of gak,
Then stagger off for aggro with the Bill,
How thou dost wish the violent eighties back!
Gone are the thrills of thy more tender day,
Now football's all just millionaires in suits
And fans would rather watch the players play
Than brickbats hurl, or stomp with bovver boots.
Though still thy heart such savagery doth crave,
The flesh is weak; thy firm hath grown infirm
And scarcely hast thou hair enough to shave;
Thy pate and paunch Time's ravages affirm.

  Take but one lesson from a life of rage:
  The most destructive hooligan is age.

# BAG FOR LIFE

Though Time upon so fleet a foot doth move,
    Though seasons shift at terrifying pace,
Though all endeavours mere diversions prove,
Though ev'ry day we further fall from grace,
Though I grow old and fashions pass me by,
Though I be raised or drowned by Fortune's wave,
Though years may dance before my rheumy eye,
Until it doth regard the restful grave,
Still shall I have thee, my companion jute;
However life — that great, unholy mess — goes,
Thou stoutly shalt encompass all the loot
Of my successive voyages to Tescos.
    (Except, of course, the nine times out of ten
    That I forget, and pay 5p again.)

# SELFIE

In modern times, Narcissus finds a pool
   Within his pocket; ev'ry pose he strikes,
Each practised pout, each look of studied cool,
Is snapped, then put on Instagram for likes.
Like Oscar's Dorian, though ancient grown
And grossly marred with liver spot and crag,
His youth shall live on in some future phone,
Which, called to screen, shall of past beauty brag.
I must confess I wince at all these snaps
And deem such onanistic pics unhealthy;
Yet, in our world of surfaces, perhaps
The height of self-expression is the selfie.
   So shoot thy visage, ere the ages spoil it,
   But prithee do not do so on the toilet.

# NAVEL LINT

My life is measured out in plugs of wool
Extracted from the darkly-wreathed lacuna
That once conjoined me to my mother; full
Of cobalt fibres is it, and no sooner
Are they pluck'd out than others doth accrue.
And as the pelage grows, so grow my queries:
Whence does it come, and wherefore is it blue?
One evening I resolve to test my theories.
I quickly find (from Google, I admit)
That scaly hairs abrade and pull within
The cotton, like to Jabba's Sarlacc pit,
Along with fat, sweat, dust, and flaked-off skin.
   (But this, I fear, is navel-gazing stuff
   And my poor sonnet just a bit of fluff.)

# EMAIL

I email her, expecting swift reply
   And yet love's message blesses not my server.
With glacial pace each hour doth trundle by,
Until my soul is gripped with manic fervour.
My heart aflame, my ev'ry synapse burning,
At least ten times a minute do I check it,
To Gmail's wretched interface returning
With all the crazed futility of Beckett.
I see from Facebook that she is online,
Thus her delay stems not from poor connection.
By now this sore and hope-strained heart of mine
Would welcome e'en the bitterest rejection.
   And so I click, till callused be my flesh:
   Refresh, refresh, refresh, refresh, refresh.

# DAVID ATTENBOROUGH

Nature's voice and nation's grandad, thou
Art our companion throughout foreign lands,
From Arctic tundra to the jungle bough,
From ocean depths to endless, scorching sands.
With tone avuncular thou dost narrate
Some ardent crab's romantic tribulation,
Then, effortless, thou lend'st thy words more weight,
Imparting knowledge of the proud cetacean.
A wondrous showman, thou tak'st care to weave
Within the majesty of thy display
A solemn message, for thou dost believe
In conservation of life's vast array.
    Ay, thou art one whose worth defies all measure:
    The lion's share of Britain's national treasure.

# TRANSFORMERS

Much like a robot from a truck unfolded,
My lady oft assumeth diff'rent guises:
One day an angel by God's own hand moulded,
The next a churl who tender thought despises.
Yet is my love no cruel Decepticon:
No malice lies in her protean art,
For unlike Starscream and vile Megatron,
No evil impulse doth control that heart.
Nay, like the valiant Autobot, these changes
Serve only to accentuate her charms;
I pray that Fate our twin souls ne'er estranges
And we grow old within each other's arms.
 Then fondly shall we look back on this time,
 When we — such optimists! — were in our prime.

# SONIC THE HEDGEHOG

How many hours of boyhood, long since fled,
   Spent I on thee, thou swift and strange-hued
   mammal,
As through those gaudy, 2D realms we sped,
The endless loops that did thy ventures trammel?
From Green Hill Zone to Scrap Brain Zone we raced,
Gold rings collecting, oft avoiding spikes;
Ne'er were thy crimson-trainered feet outpaced
No badnik e'er withstood our spinning strikes.
O azure streak, whose strong heart never truckles
To any machination of Robotnik!
Flanked by thy friends, the worthy Tails
   and Knuckles,
At thee mine eyes did stare until I got sick.
   Though manhood bids me yield such
      childish things,
   I miss those simple days of loops and rings.

# The Great British Bake Off

'Tis comfort food, and warming to my heart
    As, 'neath the watchful eyes of Mel and Sue,
The hopeful tentful hear their task and start
A frantic quest to make the perfect choux.
O world of pound cakes, pastries and politeness!
While faces change (except Paul Hollywood),
Still thou remain'st a realm of hope and brightness,
Where Britain's great and all is jolly good.
We viewers needful are of such a place:
Alas, today, our country feels half-baked;
But, in the midst of Brexit's long disgrace,
Thou, sweetest of companions, hast ne'er flaked.
    Though Fortune doth this sceptred isle forsake,
    The gods look down and say: 'Let them eat cake!'

# MAN BUN

Live and let live! I am not such a churl
As hateth hipsters for their chosen style:
When witness I the Dali moustache curl
'Pon hipster lip, I meet it with a smile.
I tremble not to see their trendy haunts,
Their coffee outlets and ironic pubs;
I have no beef with vegan restaurants,
Artistic spaces or creative hubs.
Nor loathe I tattoos crept to necks and hands,
Nor cardigans with sleeves much overgrown,
Nor references to cool and obscure bands.
'Tis but one affectation I bemoan:
    All torture's wrong, but I would gladly plan one
    For any hipster that doth sport a man bun.

# EMOJIS

Too often is the poet's pen made still
   By want of words that might his heart express,
But when love's force mine eloquence doth kill,
Technology affords me some redress.
Although my wit and tongue are rarely nimble,
I still may to my mistress love convey
Through use of some well-chosen cartoon symbol
From out my iPhone's copious array.
When loving thought into my brain-box pops,
A face with hearts for eyes may tell the story;
Meanwhile, an aubergine and water drops
Make clear I dwell on matters amatory.
   These days, the bard who claims of loving
        knows he
   Must say: 'Amo, amas, amat, emoji.'

# BATMAN

A scowl beneath a black, two-pointed cowl,
Thou dost patrol the dingy Gotham streets
And criminals who hear thy fearful growl
Will soon lament thy vigilante feats.
But why so serious, dressed like a bat?!
Thy butler's name is 'Alfred Pennyworth'!
Thine enemy's a clown! Thou think'st not that
Thy situation merits any mirth?
Thou wert not always so, thou grim Dark Knight:
Dost thou recall thy former circumstances?
When in the sixties thou wert gay and bright
And flummoxed villains with thy groovy dances?
    In spite of trendy gloom, I liked thee best
    When thou wert played, old chum, by
        Adam West.

# THE JOKER

'Twas said each actor must young Hamlet play,
But fashions change with ever-passing Time
And now it seems the role that all essay
Is Batman's foe, the dread Clown Prince of Crime.
Cesar Romero had a campy bash,
Embodying the purple-suited Pierrot,
And painted makeup o'er his own moustache,
An act to terrify the bravest hero.
A PG rating could not hope to trammel
Jack Nicholson's mad sleaze in '89.
An animated version gave Mark Hamill,
Then poor Heath Ledger did the part define.
  Each had his flaws; 'tis but one I regret, though:
  The preening pimp portrayed by Jared Leto.

# SPOTIFY

If music be the food of love, hit shuffle,
  For I would fain the grossest glutton be
And fill mine ears continually to muffle
The outside world's outrageous litany.
No anguished wail shall e'er assail my hearing
While thou art my companion, Spotify.
No yells may fright me; I shall know no sneering,
Nor harrowed be by some unholy cry,
But rather joy in thine e'er-sweet melange
Of Aphex Twin, Odd Future and The Clash;
Of Disney soundtracks, Pixies and Solange,
And of the Johnnys Rotten, Marr and Cash.
    Thus do I gladly make my daily rounds,
    Cocooned within the concord of sweet sounds.

# GOLLUM

More precious to me art thou than the ring
That did poor, tortured Smeagol so obsess;
Like him, my sole thought is that treasured thing
Torn cruelly from my covetous caress.
Emaciated lies this pallid frame
From being starved of thine addictive love,
While dwell I in a lightless cave of shame
Despising all the happy fools above.
My voice grows hoarse, my selfhood split in twain,
I crawl and hiss my bitter monologue,
Vowing that soul-craved object to regain
And, once again, her gleaming pleasures hog.
    No balrog fierce may keep me from this bliss:
    Nor orc, nor elf, nor nasty hobbitses.

# Department Store

When Christmas doth compel me through
   the doors
Of that contemp'ry palace all exult in,
Where is laid out, o'er several gleaming floors,
Such great abundance as would shame a sultan
And I survey infinities of choice
For those who can afford it — scented candles,
Pool-sized TVs, Nintendos, violent toys,
Ten brands of toenail clipper, scarves and sandals —
Then rue I capital's unholy churn,
The trinkets fashioned by some infant slave,
The want, the waste, the seas of oil we burn,
But to distract us from a looming grave.
   (That said, I fear I shall feel different when
   I have the means to buy an iPhone X.)

# ULAANBAATAR

O unknown city! How thy many vowels
Bewitch my heart and whisk my mind away;
Though I well-travelled am, thine absence howls
When this much-stampèd passport I survey.
No destination thrills me so: though Rome
Has finer food, Jerusalem is holier
And Mona Lisa doth call Paris home,
Thou dost outstrip them, pride of all Mongolia!
But still thine air has never graced my lungs,
Nor have I strode thy streets, mine eyes aflame,
Delighting in the sound of foreign tongues.
Alas, despite the music of thy name,

    I do not know thee; just what I may gauge
    From thine extensive Wikipedia page.

# PASSWORD

If there be words that might unlock thy heart,
  I know them not: like to the vital site
That needs some long-forgotten code thou art
And thus I vainly strive to end my plight.
What is thy sprawl of characters and digits,
The shibboleth I yearn to speak aloud?
Dwells it inside my documents and widgets,
Or on a keychain stored within the cloud?
Perhaps thou might some small assistance lend me,
Some subtle hint, some evanescent steer,
Or else a chance to change thy password send me;
But no, my inbox shall not feel such cheer.
  Until those magic words have I supplied,
  Thou tell'st me but one thing: access denied.

# ERECTILE DYSFUNCTION

'O burning shame! O anguish unsurpassèd!
Vile snout! Thine insolence my soul abhors:
When I am needful, thou remainest flaccid;
Wilt thou not stand for Aphrodite's cause?
A thirsting maiden lies within my bed,
Whilst I in bathroom's cell am cruelly pent.
I stroke, cajole and strike thy languid head,
Yet thou discloseth not thy least extent
But sullen hangest. Am I not thy friend?
Have I not lavished thee with tenderness?
Do I not to thine ev'ry whim attend?
So why betray me? Come, thou knave, confess!'
 My peen replies: 'I should be soon erected,
 Hadst thou, O fool, that seventh pint rejected.'

# VIAGRA

Where spirit's willing but the flesh is weak
    And hormones male hath grown unduly thin,
Deflated man may his salvation seek
By taking of a pill cerulean.
For in that hea'en-hued tablet lies the power
To galvanise the corpse 'neath thy midsection;
To reconstruct thy lately crumbled tower,
That all the world may glimpse thy proud erection.
'Tis true the wonder drug has side effects:
Insensate grows thy poor, conscripted rod,
A blushing red thy chest and throat bedecks,
Headaches and heartburn leave thee cursing God.
    But though such fearful blows some men
        may stagger,
    I gladly bear them, O thou kind Viagra!

# PICK-UP ARTIST

The hollow fool who thinketh love a game
     Some squalid cheat code for seduction seeks
And, full of slang but quite devoid of shame,
Hits up the club to try out his techniques.
He dons fedora and a statement blazer
To mock the peacock's iridescent wing;
A female corners, hoping to amaze her
With lizard tattoo or déclassé bling.
Then comes the kino, FTC and negging
And yet, for all the acronyms and jargon,
He doth remain a frightened child, just begging
For some small warmth that might his vileness
          pardon.
     Poor churl! Posterity shall ne'er survey
     A wretch so artless as the PUA.

# NEGGING

Dear sweet, I much admire thy bravery:
Thou wear'st that dress, though other girls would doubt it,
Then dost rebel 'gainst fashion's slavery
By picking shoes that do not match thine outfit.
Thy golden tresses doth bewitch the eye,
Though, looking closer, dark roots I perceive.
Thy body's good; did surgery supply
Those breasts, some vulgar fellow to deceive?
Still would I bed thee, though thy friends be finer;
Thou art a six, but I enjoy thy jests.
O, do not cry and ruin that eyeliner,
Which makes thy face less rounded when it rests!
    Egad! Why throw'st thou vodka in mine eyes?
    Come back! I guess thou likest not nice guys . . .

# ANT & DEC

When love is lost and all my dreams
lie sunken,
The bitter victims of my fortune's wreck,
Then does this fool of PJ think, and Duncan,
Or, as thou likely know'st them, Ant and Dec.
Within those Geordie Gemini a speck
Of hope I see, that hearts may loving bear;
That love may heed not dissolution's beck
But with each passing decade grow more fair.
Since they began on *Byker Grove*, the pair
Have flourished, letting not their passions ebb
And now do their presenting duties share
When torturing some jungle-based celeb.

    Therefore I pray the Lord above may grant
    That we are bonded close as Dec to Ant.

# CHRISTMAS

No blazing hearth may warm my Grinch-like
　　heart,
No lights electric can mine eye enthral,
No tints or tinsel thrill me with their art,
No angel shall I 'pon the tree install.
I shall not groove to Slade or to Mariah,
Nor wrapping paper shred with eager nails;
My groans shall prove that Scrooge was not a liar
When he deemed 'humbug' all these winter tales.
There's but one miracle that still may grant a
Degree of merriness, and it is thee;
Yet fear I e'en the most devoted Santa
Lacks power to deliver thee to me.
　　Thus I, poor wretch, shall ne'er find
　　　　Yuletide pleasant
　　Unless thou art, my love, this Christmas present.

# WILLIAM SHAKESPEARE

## *1.*

Will you forgive me, Will, for willing these
   Dumb verses to existence? From the noise
Of modern life I wished some sense to tease,
Then make it sweet with this, your sacred voice.
But never would I wish that voice defiled:
You are my idol, writer ne plus ultra;
I breathed your rhymes since I was but a child,
Your rhythm forms the heartbeat of my culture.
Yet now I see these sonnets bear no beauty:
Their subjects are sarcastic, nerdy, niche;
My trifling wit has dodged the poet's duty
And wasted readers' time with pale pastiche.
   Will, I confess my resolution breaks here:
   What right has this weak will to pose as
      Shakespeare?

## 2.

Still, all these self-aimed insults I should leaven,
For Will, with all the will in this wide world,
You were no god, your words came not from heaven,
Like lightning from Olympus' summit hurled.
Some of your sonnets suck: you had bad days.
Sometimes your song's a ditty, not a hymn
(See 145). And that Dark Lady phase?
You sound like Eminem discussing Kim.
But I would have you flawed: the world's true poet
Must, as the world, be earthy and sublime
And by example of his error show that
It shames us not to err from time to time,

    For master weavers know their small mistake
    May some new unsuspected beauty make.

## 3.

You were a man in Tudor times, who drank
      Ten pints of beer a day, who whores did know,
Who took no baths, whose body doubtless stank,
Who tipped his pail of shit on streets below;
Who got some woman pregnant, and then fled
To plash the endless mire of London town
And set his mind to please those common-bred
Who joyed in murder, wolfed each dick joke down.
But from that dirty mind, those reeking lips,
Which yellow, rotting teeth were hid behind,
Came words that did antiquity eclipse:
Undying music of celestial kind.
      Not of an age, but for all Time were you
      (Some of those dick jokes were quite funny, too).

## 4.

Fie on those fools who say you are not you
And would your Will revoke; be they accursed
Who would on Oxford's earl your laurels strew,
Or even Queen Elizabeth the First!
Whene'er I hear their wretched argument,
My mind soon turns to Jacobean violence,
For reasoned discourse cannot hope to dent
The confidence of Jacobi or Rylance.
I fear the root of this conspiracy
Is mere disdain for you, a glover's son.
They ask: 'How could a man of such degree
Have tapestries of such great wonder spun?'
    But we both know that posh boys get defensive:
    You went to grammar school; I, comprehensive.

## 5.

You liked to liken all sorts to the sun,
So for your genius will I do the same:
Around your wit succeeding wits have spun
And none succeeded to eclipse your fame.
Just as the sun can warm our human skin
Across the vast and frosty field of Space,
So too I feel your heat; our hearts are kin,
Though centuries divide me from your grace.
But you were not divine; no, just a man
Who made his soul a mirror to our world,
Who dwelt among us, and, for all his span,
To ev'ry eye unearthly brilliance hurled.
Thus Will, your golden radiance will endure
As long as minds can race and hearts can soar.

# ACKNOWLEDGEMENTS

The blame for all of this is mine; what praise
My book doth merit goes to those dear souls
Who made it happen, saw me through dark days
And strove to plug my learning's many holes:
My comrade Ollie, the Renaissance Mann
Whose gorgeous lines my own lines doth enhance,
My editors, who steered me with elan
Through publishing's insanely complex dance,
My parents, for their never-ending patience,
And Dr Zurcher, for his knowledge vast,
My pledgers kind, plus ev'ry vague acquaintance
Who, for their hard-earned money, I harassed
And, finally, the one to whom is due
My love and thanks eternal: you-know-Hu.

# ABOUT THE AUTHOR

Thy poet was in northern England born,
Upon the Geordie Shore in '88.
He spent his adolescent years forlorn,
Bereft of hope that he might find a mate.
But reading Shakespeare's verse, it did occur
To him that he should master sonnetry
And write some stanzas to a fancied her,
Escaping thus his cruel virginity!
Of course, that did not happen: they were shit
And, filled with shame, the lad set down his quill,
Then left his teens with naught to show for it,
Beyond a new and truly pointless skill.
    So now he doth, in quasi-comic guise,
    Attempt his wasted youth to monetise.

Unbound is the world's first crowdfunding publisher, established in 2011.

We believe that wonderful things can happen when you clear a path for people who share a passion. That's why we've built a platform that brings together readers and authors to crowdfund books they believe in – and give fresh ideas that don't fit the traditional mould the chance they deserve.

This book is in your hands because readers made it possible. Everyone who pledged their support is listed below. Join them by visiting unbound.com and supporting a book today.

Abigail Barclay
Daisy Bard
Adam Bargroff
Seb Barwell
Kellie Batchelor
Alison Baverstock
Jim Baxter
Alix Beale
Victoria Beale
Emma Bell
Greg Beres
Jack Bernhardt
Ella Berthoud
Lydia Bewley
Karan Bhatt
Sarah Bibby
Matthew Blackett
Rebecca Bleach
Claudia Blunt
Martin Bojam
Peter Bowden
Joe Brennan
Andrew Brereton
Nathan Brooker
Harriet Elizabeth Brown
Russell Bruns
Sam Bryant

Francis Bull
Clare Bullock
Claire Burridge
Adam Byron
John Callen
Rob Carter
Chuck Caruso
James Cary
Prof. Susan Chambers,
    PhD (Cantab.)
Andrew Chapman
Tim Checkley
Ken Cheng
Thomas Chigbo
Jo Clark
Sue Clark
Nathalie Clarke
Sophie Clarke
Reginald Clovis
Lawrence Cochran
Gina Cocking
Dave Cohen
Richard Cook
Lauren Cooney
Mark E Cooper
Jenna Corderoy
Emina Cosic

Katy Costello

Robert Cox

Sophie Dalling

Jessica Dannheisser

Vivian Darkbloom

Colin Davey

Richard Davies

Zygmunt Day

Sharon Dean

Mary Devereux

Greg Dickens

Peter Dickinson

Wendalynn Donnan

Lizzie Donnelly

Charlotte Doolan

Paul Doolan

Ciaran Dowd

Alan Dowsing

Mareta Doyle

Adam Drew

Aaron Duncan

D.G. Duncan

Seb Eastham

Phoebe Eclair-Powell

Gareth Edwards

Humphrey Elles-Hill

Beth Elliott

Joe Evans

Lucy Evans

Mark Evans

Matthew Evans

Lucy Eyre-Tanner

James Farrell & Adam Kay

Jessica Fell

Saima Ferdows

Manolita Foster

Lynda Fothergill

Elizabeth Francis

Alice Fraser

Matthew Fraser

Robin French

Fred Friedman

Stephen Fry

Paco B. Garcia

Tom George

Manjit Ghattaura

Patricia Gibbons

Mel Giedroyc

Phil Gilbert

Iván González

Meg Gordon Sussman

Clare Walker Gore

Richard Granby

Josh Green

Sarah Grieves
Cathy Griffiths
Cicely Hadman
Greg Haiste
Marc Kevin Hall
Will Hall
Sarah Halliday
Sarah Hammond
Joe Harris
Kevin Hayward
Zoah Hedges-Stocks
Verity Henderson
Chris Heppell
Katya Herman
Dan Hine
Sophie Hodge
Kieran Hodgson
Robyn Hoedemaker
Amy Hoggart
Louisa Hollway
Liam Hourican
D. P. Howard-Jones
Mengxi Hu
Matt Hulme
Alana Hutton-Shaw
David Isaacs
Laura Jellicoe

Hannah Jenkins
Jessica Jennings
Marjorie Johns
Daran Johnson
Melissa Johnson
Lizzy Johnstone
Hattie Jones
Ralph Jones
Tom Jordan
Joseph Kay
Amy Kean
Peg Keller
Kate Kennard
Emer Kenny
Dan Kieran
Matt Kilroy
Patrick Kincaid
The King's School Library
Tom Kingsley
Chris Knott
Felicity Lane
Sam Laolu
The Last Crumb Café
Adam Lawrence
Daniella Lebor
Giles Lesser
Eleanor Lewis

Johndy Lewis
Jenny Lindfors
Thomas Lloyd-Evans
Elliott Louis
David Lowry
Thomas Lyle
Ed MacArthur
Vladimir Makarov
Sue Maloney
Janie Mann
Mann Mann
Joe Markham
Julia Markus
Matthew Marsh
David Matkins
Nicola McCaffrey
Elly McCausland
Thomas McCluskey
Iain McCoy
Felicity McKay
Aidan McQuade
Harry Michell
Bryan Mitchell
John Mitchinson
Tom Moody-Stuart
James Moran
Frank Moriarty

Anna Mrowiec
Rory Mullarkey
Fionán Mulvihill
Jimmy Mulville
Johan Munir
Katie Murphy
Chandkiran Nath
Simon Nathan
Carlo Navato
Zac Newman
Thomas Newton
Phil Norris
Mairin O'Hagan
Brian O'Malley
Katie Ogilvie
Max Olesker
Alice Orr-Ewing
Naz Osmanoglu
Emily, Jon and Axl Owen
Libby Page
Sebastian Palmer
Thomas Palmer
Joe Parham
Emerald Paston
Priti Patel
Frank Paul
Lyndall Pauna

Bertie Peek

Thom Phipps

Justin Pollard

Lara Prendergast

Sharron Preston

Ruben Quesada

Kieron Quirke

Ploy Radford

Dharmesh Rajput

Duam Rallim

Johnny Really-Really

Tim Reid

Maura Reidy

Mark Reisman

Aaron Reynolds

Nick Ricketts

Liam Riley

Charlotte Ritchie

Al Roberts

Tony Roberts

Danny Robins

Abigail Rokison-Woodall

Amy Rose

Stewart Ross

Stephanie Rouse

Simon Rowbotham

Nancy Rowe

Ben Rowse

Jamie Russell

Ian Samson

Elena Santamaria

Rosanna Seal

Jacob Sharpe

James Sharpe

Michael Sherley-Dale

Raph Shirley

Jules Skelding

Emma Smith

Fraser Smith

Akiva Solemani

Hannah Solemani

Avril Spary

Henry Staples

Henriette B. Stavis

Alison Steel

James Steel

John Steel

Peter Steel

Rick Steele

Matt Steer

Catriona Stirling

Frog Stone

Tom Stourton

Chris Sussman

Frederick Syborn
Cat Sylvain
James Syrett
Louise Taylor
Melissa Taylor
Neil Xavier Taylor
Miranda Thewlis
Steven Thomas
Brona C Titley
Joy Tuffield
Melinda Underwood
Imola Unger
Amandeep Uppal
Max Upton
Carlos Velez
Mark Vent
Derran Venus
Lucy Vickery
Lauren Walden
Kitty Walsh
Phil Wang
Sam Ward
Anne Warmington
Steve Warmington
Julie Warren
Leah Wasacz
James Watson-O'Neill

Susan Wear
Will Weiner
Alexandra Welsby
Henry White
Joel White
Taia White
Peter Wilkinson
Kate Williams
Liam Williams
Tom Williams
Simon Wilson
Sophie Wilson
Alexander Winterbotham
Katy Wix
Matilda Wnek
Lauren Workman
Henry Wriothesley
Charlotte Wylie
Phil Yeeles
Benjamin Yeoh
Alison Young
Frankie Young
Marjorie Young
Philip Young
Laura Zederkof
Dan Zeff